GARY SINCLAIR

NOW!!

Breaking Free From The
Someday Syndrome

Thanks!

[signature]

Gary Sinclair

Published by *Never Quit Climbing,* Indianapolis, Indiana with support from TCK Publishing.com

To the colleagues, friends, teachers and
family who I have worked with and loved over
the years and have encouraged me to not wait until
tomorrow to do what God is asking of me today.

Gary Sinclair

TABLE OF CONTENTS

INTRODUCTION

I have to tell the truth. I'm sorry to say that I've avoided completing NOW for the last couple of decades. I've crafted version after version, title after title, contacted publishers and told hundreds, maybe thousands, that I was writing it. Still there was always some reason it wasn't finished. I could bore you with reasons but you don't care and I would just be trying to look less culpable.

As you can imagine, I am thrilled that you are finally getting to read the finished product. But, while I've completed other projects in the meantime, I've been somewhat paralyzed or at best stuck on this one.

Why? Well, it's due in part to a debilitating condition that I call the *Someday Syndrome*. It's the focus of this book.

At one point, I was going to complete this work after our kids got older. A later benchmark was to first move, then after I finished grad school, when I finally nailed down my next job and more recently after I published any one of my other three books. They are available online now. Whew!

But there was always one more reason why I couldn't get the final product finished. Can you relate? Please tell me you can. The problem is that our reasons for pushing

1

important things into the future are many, complex and often subtle in their manifestation.

In *NOW,* I want to help you finally overcome the pull of someday and become who God wants you to be in the present. Yes, some things should wait and I'll talk about that too.

The good news is that I'm quite sure the book's content has improved over the years because my thinking has matured. I am definitely a better writer today so that should count for something, right?

My understanding of living *NOW* has deepened and simmered, so hopefully you're getting a much better, more refined, very practical and passionate book.

However, I want to be clear that I know how easy it is to get sucked into the *Someday Syndrome,* driven by a host of things that keeps people from moving forward. I understand what it's like to relegate goals, dreams, hopes and big plans to later, to a more convenient, expeditious time, to a *someday* that is always looming.

Someday. What does that word conjure up in you?

Maybe you're remembering back to elementary school when you dreamed of being in the Olympics or playing for a professional team. Or you're the college student hoping to meet your one and only, imagining you will be married to someone you couldn't live without. Or you're a middle-aged empty-nester who longs for the day when you'll have that first grandbaby.

Somedays aren't necessarily bad or wrong. In fact, they usually overflow with hope, anticipation and wishful excitement. And yet, for many, *someday* is also a curse, a self-imposed hex that prevents them from moving forward to embrace needed and longed-for change. It means that their commitment to be who they were meant to be is but a foggy fantasy that may never happen.

September 11th, 2001, will forever be imprinted on the hearts of those of us old enough to remember it. The images of the *World Trade Center* buildings crashing to the ground as thousands were ushered into eternity will haunt us until the day we die.

And yet, while the magnitude of the tragedy that day will never be fully realized, some of us wondered if 9/11 would serve as a wake-up call to the world, a painful cry of, "*Quit sleeping! Don't you get it? It's time to take inventory, to start thinking about what really matters!*"

In fact, the Sunday after 9/11 churches in America typically saw huge increases in attendance. There were spontaneous prayer services involving thousands who sought answers from at least a higher power.

All across the country, pastors, while attempting to salve wounds and speak words of comfort, challenged people to renew commitments to live for Christ and to become His radical followers.

But mere months later, church attendance returned to its former numbers. While sacrificial giving, volunteerism and ministry opportunities surged for a time, the demand to live comfortably lured many to a false sense of normalcy.

As I edit this chapter, our country and world are being besieged, overwhelmed and in many ways upended by the Coronavirus. In spite of vaccinations and more testing than ever, families still face unknowns and changes never experienced befor.

Many are out of work, at least temporarily, and don't know when their job or some sense of normalcy will return. It's another 911 minus the terrorism as far as we know.

It could be a similar motivator for millions to live differently, to revisit what's most important and become who they could be instead of what everyone else wants them to be. In fact, some are making radical changes right now, ones they really couldn't avoid.

Nonetheless, it's my premise that a significant number of well-meaning Christians, leaders of churches, helpers, every-Sunday worshippers and self-described followers of

Christ have lapsed into what Jesus describes in Luke chapter 9 and what I am calling in this book, *The Someday Syndrome*. And so far, major tragedies, challenges and disasters only cause significant change for a short time.

The Someday Syndrome is the mindset that leads many to say, "*I'll eventually give Christ my whole life and I will change, I will risk becoming all I can be for God, I will become a better father, mother, friend or person in general, but I can't do it right now.*"

As a result, many sacrifice their mental health, avoid new levels of marital harmony, suffer emotional malfunction or in some other way delay the opportunity to live in a new way or better themselves significantly.

If that describes you, even in small measure, then this book is for you. Thanks for your willingness to come along on this journey of exploration and discovery. I have been where you are and am still learning about *NOW* living.

But if you've put many endeavors off to *someday,* then I hope you'll keep reading with an open mind, with the goal of grasping what you've missed by not living *NOW* and might enjoy up ahead.

In spite of my procrastination on this work, I am not a person who generally lives in the *someday* anymore. In fact, that's why I felt like I needed to finish what I started.

During my *somedays,* I've looked at myself with the help of several wise counselors and writers and figured out why I was stuck. I've also worked for years as a coach, minister and confidante for people who are emotionally paralyzed and never move forward to do what they could do and be who they could be.

They rarely live in joy, happiness and fulfillment. There's always something that has to happen first. Sadly, many of these same people die leaving their goals, dreams, hopes and possibilities behind.

Fortunately, I've been able to help some of them get un-stuck and move their goals, passions and needed changes from *somewhere* in the distance to NOW.

They've learned to overcome their fears and deal with the inner struggle that has kept them stagnant and move to a life that goes after dreams and becomes what God knew they could be. I'll share key concepts and first steps you can take to also move from *someday* to NOW.

Naturally, I'm not suggesting that everything we seek to do or become should be accomplished right away. I'll talk more in a later chapter about how to decide to wait.

But my purpose here is to help get you off the dime. I want to challenge you to move forward and take steps NOW to live differently, to deal with issues that need your attention, to overcome difficulties that perhaps you thought were impossible to tackle and to grow to maturity *NOW!*

But unfortunately, the list of potential *somedays* is long. Millions are waiting for tomorrow while God is begging them to embrace His purposes today. As we'll see in the upcoming chapters, there are several common replies to God's prodding such as, *"But first I have to do something or something else must happen before I can move forward."*

The memories and impact of 9/11 may have faded and the Coronavirus will wane, but will whatever motivates us to move forward remain a lifestyle not a phase. Life can end in a moment's notice, sometimes in ways we never expected. No one is guaranteed 70+ years.

Our being young or old is not about how many years we have lived but rather how many years we have left!

That means that there are times when waiting, being patient and allowing time for more preparation are necessary before we tackle a new venture or stage of growth. What are you putting off to tomorrow that could be done or at least started *NOW?*

I'll try to help you examine and understand hidden fears, agendas, misguided thinking and other hindrances that may be holding you back. I'll give you practical ideas for what to do next that will move your lifestyle from tomorrow thinking to appropriate *NOW* actions.

Read slowly and expectantly. Stop and review the questions at the end of each chapter. Ponder, think and look deeply into your heart and soul. It's there that you'll discover many of the roadblocks in your way, ones that keep you from *NOW* living.

You have the potential to discover a freedom, excitement and joy about life that *someday* could never give you. Get started and begin to discover what living *NOW* might look and feel like. You'll never want to go back.

As a people helper, I am well aware that authentic change is usually slow and deliberate. I'm not advocating a lets-suck-it-up-and-just-get-going attitude or merely a power of positive thinking approach to life. Genuine change is not easy and that's okay.

But with God's help, you can become free of the someday paralysis that has robbed you of life in the present. Join me on the road to becoming a person who is making a difference right *NOW!* Read on.

SOMEDAY AND SECURITY
CHAPTER 1

"It's not how much we have, but how much we enjoy, that makes happiness." Charles Spurgeon

Putting things off is hardly a new phenomenon. What I call the *Someday Syndrome* has been around since people first walked the earth. We have always been procrastinating and settling for superficial change, armed with myriad excuses as to why we can't be different or move forward.

The Bible is stocked with examples of godly saints who elicited their own faulty arguments for why they couldn't follow God's plan for their lives. One of the clearest descriptions of mankind's penchant for putting things off can be found in Luke 9:57-60.

Let me set the stage for you.

Jesus is approaching the final days of his early ministry. James and John, two of His favorite trainees and companions at the *Transfiguration*, seem to sense the impending difficulties as they make arrangements for Jesus' travel to the Holy City. While on their way, however, they receive a less than cordial welcome from the Samaritans (Luke 9:51-56).

In response, the dynamic duo offers to play bodyguards for Jesus and call down fire from Heaven, thinking they could borrow power from Elijah who they had just encountered on the mountain.

Instead, Jesus urges them on toward the next village. Somewhere along the way they begin a discussion about the future, possibly debating who was going to have the courage to stick with Jesus if things got rough.

Three individuals (as far as we know) now enter the narrative. It's likely that several of them were other disciples or lesser known followers who had joined them for this segment of the journey. Their comments and Jesus' responses nonetheless provide us with a trilogy of fascinating scenarios found in Luke 9:57-62.

The first respondent appears to have been eager to join the Jesus Team and blurts out, *"I will follow you wherever you go." (v. 57)* But Jesus replies in v. 58, *"The foxes have holes, and the birds of the air have nest, but the Son of Man has nowhere to lay His head."*

The second, having also been urged by Jesus to, *"Follow me,"* enters the conversation and states, *"Lord, first let me go and bury my father,"* (v. 59) The man seems genuinely interested but apparently felt his family concerns needed immediate attention.

Jesus, in what had to have been viewed as a most curious statement by this promising follower, replied, *"Let the dead bury their own dead: but you go and proclaim the kingdom of God."* (v. 60) The third person from the entourage, also eager to make a positive impression and perhaps hoping to outshine the second guy, says, *"I will follow you Lord; but first let me go back and say good-bye to my family." (v. 61)*

However, Jesus again responded somewhat harshly, "No one who puts his hand to the plow and looks back is fit for service in the kingdom of God."

In each case, Jesus was well aware that living for *someday* would inhibit these disciples from genuine, committed involvement in following Him. They had not come to the place where they were willing to give everything. Jesus knew that the human heart tends to seek its own comfort and ease rather than the trials of long-term service or sacrifice.

Biblical Examples of Someday Living

Jesus was no doubt aware of historical Bible figures who had clung to their own somedays before making a serious commitment to God. Remember Abraham and Sarah, clearly too old in human terms to have a child, even though one had been promised to them?

Upon hearing God's supernatural plan for him and Sarah, Abraham immediately considered other alternatives, *"Oh, that Ishmael might live before Thee,"* he pleaded.

But God's intentions were not to be stopped. Age, circumstances, and the parameters of the human body were no obstacle for Him. *"Yes, but Sarah your wife will bear you a son, and you shall call him Isaac; I will establish my covenant with him as an everlasting covenant for his descendants after him."* *(Genesis 17:19, 20)*

Or many years later, even after the Lord explains that He will be Moses' mouth for him, Moses begs that someone else do the speaking. *"O, Lord, please send someone else to do it."* (Exodus 4:13)

Likewise, Saul chosen by God to be the first king of Israel, balked at God's challenge from the very beginning, wondering if he was ready for his royal assignment. Before Samuel ever anoints him, Saul responds apologetically: *'But I am not a Benjamite, from the smallest tribe of Israel, and is not my clan the least of all the clans of the tribe of Benjamin? Why do you say such a thing to me?"* (I Samuel 9:21)

Who can help but chuckle when we think of this huge man hiding behind the baggage on the day of his announcement as king? Saul had been chosen to be God's anointed one and the Holy Spirit had come upon him mightily. Nonetheless, he was afraid to follow God wholeheartedly. What was he waiting for?

Another someday syndrome captive was the Old Testament prophet Jeremiah who told God: *"Ah Sovereign Lord, I do not know how to speak; I am only a child."* *(Jeremiah*

1:6) Or in more colloquial terms, *"Someday, Lord, when I get older, I can speak for you, but please not now."*

In contrast, Mary, Jesus' earthly mother, a prime candidate for her own *Someday Club*, chose not to wait. Astonished, she heard the unbelievable news that she was to be the matriarch of the Messiah's family. Her fair question, *"How will this be?"* (Luke 1:34) illustrates her understandable wonder at the realization that an innocent, adolescent Jewish girl like herself would be used by God as the focal point of the most incredible birth in history!

Thankfully, Mary, even in her naïve uncertainty, declares, *"May it be to me as you have said."* (Luke 1:38) She was not about to wait for tomorrow or the next day or the next to be the most famous mom ever!

A Child-like Attitude

It is critical to note Jesus' reminders that we must come to Him with child-like faith. What Christian's heart strings have not been touched by the picture of Him with the little children laughing, sitting on His lap, enjoying Him in all His gentle, God-filled humanity? Jesus never would have said to those little ones, *"Come back to me SOMEDAY when you are older, more mature, more knowledgeable."*

He loved children in all their innocence, wrapping His strong, loving arms around them, eager for them to stay.

It is this same Jesus, with His love and supernatural wisdom, who made sure that each of Luke 9's would-be followers knew the challenges ahead if they committed to Him.

My hunch is that if you regularly work with people as a pastor, teacher, or counselor you can think of similar individuals who hold tightly to excuses as to why they can't commit. Or maybe you've met people led to full-time Christian work who won't take even a first step to pursue it. Could one of those waiting for a similar *someday* be YOU?

The Point of No Return

I am an airplane junkie, wannabe pilot and lover of airports. Whenever I fly, I like to watch aircraft land and take off. If I'm on a flight sitting near a window, I'm captivated by what's down below.

I can spout off the subtle differences in most commercial jets and if I had the money, I would get my pilot's license in a heartbeat! Anyone who offers me an opportunity to fly gets an immediate *yes* in response.

While studying airplanes, however, I learned an interesting fact that even many frequent fliers are oblivious to. The pilots and their computers have mathematically determined an unseen line on the runway which is colloquially known as *the point of no return*. It's the place where once the plane of its size, weight, and type passes, it MUST take off.

Thankfully, the passengers are never told that! Can you imagine the pilot or flight attendant saying over the PA system while the plane is hurtling down the runway, *"Ladies and gentlemen, sit back and relax? We have just passed the point of no return!"*

Nevertheless, the line does exist. When the plane reaches a point known as, "V1," the pilots know they must commit to the takeoff no matter what happens. There isn't enough runway left at that point to stop safely.

Unfortunately, many people live life on the safe side of a similar line, waiting, conjuring up excuses, unwilling to risk going past their *point of no return*. Deep within them lies a yearning to serve God with the gifts He has given them. However, their hopes, dreams and possibility of accomplishing great things often get stuffed into the recesses of their mind.

Gary Sinclair

They know there is more to life and could soar and seek out bold, new challenges and opportunities.

Yet somehow for these people the magnitude of the risk wins though every time a plane takes off there's a risk.

Jesus experienced this same tension as he counseled the disciples along the road. As we'll see He invites them to walk toward that risk with Him. In fact, it's their discussions that guide our thinking throughout the rest of this book. Let's look at the first encounter.

The Someday of *Securities*

Whether Jesus initially said anything to the individual in his first encounter is unknown, but it is possible that He may have said, *"Follow me,"* as he did with the second person who we'll look at next. Nonetheless, this potential follower's response was a seemingly enthusiastic, *"I will follow you wherever you go."* He apparently believed he would passionately pursue Christ no matter what and wherever He went.

Sounds impressive, doesn't it? Chances are he would have eagerly walked the aisle during a dedication service, had tears streaming down his cheeks or confidently raised his hand or signed a response card at church after the pastor's invitation. He probably appeared to be ready to leave with the Master right then and there!

Jesus, however, heard both the man's heart and his words, responding with what had to be a very curious and certainly unexpected statement. *"Foxes have holes and birds of the air have nests but the Son of Man has no place to lay His head." (9:58)*

Say what? This guy had to be wondering, "I've just committed myself to missionary service under the Messiah and He's telling me about the lack of homes within the fox and bird population?"

12

At that, many would have wondered if Jesus was really some religious wanderer spouting off spiritual-sounding maxims while totally out of touch with reality.

But Jesus' response was far more profound than this optimistic follower could have imagined. Note the two key words here: *holes* and *nests*. To animals particularly, the fox and the bird in this case, holes and nests are places of comfort, rest and safety. Birds will literally spend days, even weeks building a dwelling place for themselves and their little ones.

A number of years ago a feathered friend in our neighborhood decided to construct a nest in the family mailbox. For weeks and weeks that determined sparrow would faithfully add to her family's lodging in spite of my daily purging of all her hard work (please, no texts or nasty emails.)

But somehow the winged parent instinctively knew the importance of a safe and secure home and what it means to the rest of her family. She wasn't about to give up her creature comforts and security without a fight! Maybe you too have experienced a similar appreciation of home after an extended trip when you were finally able to snuggle into your own bed again.

Children, like baby birds, are especially impacted when they've been separated for a time from their home. I will never forget how Tim, then two years old, reacted when we returned to Michigan after ten weeks in Dallas where I was attending seminary for the summer. Before Jackie and I could even get our luggage unloaded and into the house, Tim disappeared.

When we went to look for him, guess where he was! He was sitting in the middle of his bed with the biggest smile repeating the word, *"Home, home, home."* He was in safe territory again and at that moment there was no place like it!

What was Jesus referring to that would keep this first candidate for the discipleship team from dropping everything and being a total follower of Christ? In today's terms we would call it *Security*. Like most people he wanted assurances that life would keep on as it always did.

In our culture that often means a nice place to live, enough money in the bank, the right job, substantially more education, a retirement plan, all the bills paid or a thousand other security-producing assets. But Jesus knew that the man's preoccupation with future comforts and social stability would drastically impinge on his willingness to serve God with all his heart.

Material security

Recent blatant terrorist attacks around the world and the recent,. tragic virus spread have made us even more insecure about our safety. When professional athletes are questioned about their exorbitant salaries they often respond, "*I just want security for my family.*" When we make a major purchase, we want to be sure it has a guarantee or hefty warranty, don't we?

Many of us still hope that the government's pre-pay plan for retirement called *Social Security* exists by the time we retire. Measures to keep our information safe are always being refined and updated as unscrupulous people keep trying to sneak into our accounts and resources.

Obviously, *financial security* in and of itself isn't a bad thing. There's nothing wrong with wisely and efficiently planning for the future with the idea that there will be resources on hand when they are needed. Saving for college, retirement, health needs and even a special trip is unquestionably wise. Jesus Himself spoke about counting the cost ahead of time, whether in building structures or fighting battles. (Luke 14: 25-35)

The problem for most of us is that we want to believe that there will come a time when we are completely secure, at least here on earth, and unfortunately that is a pipe dream. God never promised us that the material possessions we have today will be here tomorrow.

Just as the twin towers in New York city toppled in an agonizing instant, so our resources can be gone in the twinkling of an eye.

I spent several days in southern Mississippi and saw firsthand the incredible damage and destruction that Hurricane Katrina did. Both the wealthy and the poor lost everything. The destruction did not favor any one class of people.

Material security for thousands was stolen by one powerful storm in a matter of hours. More recently there has been terrible flooding in the Midwest that has ruined millions of dollars of property and possessions.

Proverbs speaks about the false sense of security that materialism affords. *"The wealth of the rich is their fortified city, they imagine it an unscalable wall."* *(18:11)* In the 1940s, our country was still in the depths of hardship, enduring soup kitchens, the closings of banks, and long lines. Ironically, President Franklin Roosevelt, urged the people on with these insightful words, *"Our difficulties, thank God, concern only material things."*

How sad to realize that scores of people in our churches and cities today are waiting for their lives to seem more secure before they will step forward to serve Christ or embrace personal change. Many say, *"Lord, I'll be glad to serve once I get my education finished."* Or *"God, don't you understand? We don't even own our own home and you want us to cut back on work so we can do ministry?"*

"Once I get that promotion my time will be more my own and I can get involved in a Bible study . . ." or tackling key political issues . . . or serving on a missions' team . . . or getting my marriage back together or . . . spending quality time with the kids."

J. Paul Getty, at one time the richest man in the world, was once asked how much money it took for him to be happy or satisfied. His answer was simple, but profound. *"Just a little bit more."*

Perhaps part of our reluctance to move forward during insecure times is that we don't really understand where our security comes from in the first place. The dictionary defines security as: *"Freedom from apprehension; confidence of safety; freedom from danger or risk."*

Unfortunately, we are never totally free from anxiety about life. We aren't always safe. Danger and risk are always lurking. We live with security levels, terrorism, pandemics, economic ups and downs and increasing violence.

Sure, there are those who suggest we can claim God's protection or provision, but most people who hold that view admit their lives are still insecure. Their children get sick at times, financial needs still come their way, people they know die before their time.

A financial consultant I heard some years ago told the story of house-sitting for six months for friends who lived in a half-million-dollar-plus home. Living there was a HUGE step up from his own house and it was a special luxury just to stay there.

However, the day came when his time in what he considered a mansion was over and he headed back to his modest, middle class dwelling place. Several friends asked him, *"Wasn't it hard to leave that beautiful home with all its amenities and return to your everyday home?"*

"Yes, it was a little difficult," he responded, *"but it was a lot easier to leave when I remembered that it didn't belong to me in the first place."*

Our material possessions have never belonged to us. We have them only by the grace of God. They are on loan but only temporarily. We are house-sitting them for a time. But if we keep remembering that what we have was never really ours, then of course it's easier to let go of it or even give it back.

Physical security

In addition to all the comforts of home, Americans also place increasing importance on their appearance and health. Employees now work out on their lunch hours and some larger churches provide aerobics, exercise facilities and fitness plans. Runners and walkers hardly get a second look as they whiz through our neighborhoods, malls and parks or head into the 24-hour workout options.

As *Baby Boomers* age we do everything possible to still feel like and look like we're only thirty-five. *Facebook* and other online ads are filled with the latest ways to bulk up, slim down, be sexier and generally look younger.

In fact, more and more young people are turning to plastic surgery to fix chins and increase or reduce breasts. Teenage boys will risk their reproductive potential and marital happiness by eagerly downing steroids to acquire more dramatic increases in muscle size. One young man quoted in Sports Illustrated said, *"The improvements I achieved using steroids made me more popular."*

And we know that exercise and general care for our bodies IS good for us. We would be a healthier country if more of us got off the couch and onto the treadmill every day. Many of our kids need to put down the video game controller and get some exercise. But can we ever enjoy total physical security?

Joni Eareckson Tada, paralyzed years ago through a diving accident as a teenager, probably understands life's physical uncertainties better than most of us. The seeming security of physical health and adolescent energy was snatched from her in one careless act, leaving her with a keen, brilliant mind, imprisoned in a body no longer in her control.

And yet through it all, God over the years painted for her a bigger picture of life. In her book *Choices, Changes,* she pens these insightful words:

"This wheelchair has helped me sit still. I observed with curiosity the way we Christians grasp for the future, as if the present didn't quite satisfy. How we, in spiritual fits and starts, scrape and scratch our way along, often missing the best of life while looking the other way, preoccupied with shaping our future."

It was just before the Thanksgiving and Christmas holidays some thirteen years ago that my wife Jackie called me after what was to be a check-up with a specialist. She'd had some bleeding, but eighteen months before she had also had a colonoscopy and we were told everything looked good. The bleeding, the doctor speculated, was likely from some previously diagnosed problems and the specialist would probably confirm that.

She and our daughter Amy went off to what appeared to be a routine appointment. Instead, the doctor told Jackie that she had a tumor in her rectum and he was 90% sure it was cancer. *Security?* We had climbed a 14er in Colorado just a couple of months before. The church seemed to be doing well.

Other than some arthroscopic surgery on my shoulder, neither of us had been in the hospital for anything! Suddenly, our physical security was teetering. (I've written our story, the principles learned and the journey it took us on in my book, *Never Quit Climbing: Overcoming Life's Seemingly Insurmountable Mountains.*)

The only source of true security, God, never promised us a cake walk through life. Material, physical and financial security with a lifetime guarantee isn't ever going to happen. If that is what we're waiting for before we'll serve God or truly change, we have a long wait. In fact, our only option is to hold out for death or Christ to come back!

However, the Bible does speak about how our personhood, our value as an individual, and our relationship with God are always secure. There's no event, shortcoming or hurtful experience that has the power to destroy our standing as a child in His family.

Our place in His household does come with a lifetime guarantee. Where many go wrong is believing that God also warranties our personal happiness and pleasure in this life.

Psychologist Larry Crabb used to say in one of his counseling classes, *"There are no 100-foot drops in this life, only three-foot ones."* I love to sport climb and climb mountains. I'm not a professional but I enjoy a challenge. Friends and I used to climb sixty-five-foot walls with only a rope and a harness keeping us from falling to our deaths. Dropping from those heights is typically fatal.

In contrast, we can get hurt from a three-foot fall but that would rarely cause death. But if we think of our trials and hardships as hundred-foot drops, then yes, we would anticipate the worst. If not having material or physical security feels to us like a hundred-foot drop then we'll do everything we can to hold on to it for dear life.

The good news is that in God's eyes our personhood can never die. Do we deserve His love and our place in God's family? Of course not. There is no way we could have ever earned it in the first place. God's grace gives us what we don't deserve.

"By this I know that God is for me. In God, whose word I praise, in the Lord whose word I praise — In God I trust; I will not be afraid. What can man do to me?" (Psalm 56:9ff)

Our deep desires to make a difference, to be loved and to find meaning will only be fulfilled in God Himself. Listen again to David in Psalm 63: 1-5 express his yearnings to God:

"My soul thirsts for you, my body longs for you, in a dry and weary land where there is no water. I have seen you in the sanctuary and beheld your power and your glory.

Because your love is better than life, my lips will glorify you. I will praise you as long as I live, and in your name I will lift up my hands. My soul will be satisfied as with the richest of foods; with singing lips my mouth will praise you."

Security apart from God is a fairy tale, a hoax, fake news. To try to find permanent stability and unconditional money-back guarantees in this world is like trying to hold on to fog. Real security comes from knowing that you can never lose your value, status and purpose in God's eyes.

You and I have been made with a purpose, to soar, to be all that God crafted us to be. Yes, we are stained and tainted by our selfishness, but we are loved by God because of the death and resurrection of Jesus Christ on that first Easter weekend.

As trekkers climbing up God's mountain, we must grasp that security is not something to be attained but a precious gift we already possess!

If we are waiting to change in some significant and necessary way or hesitating to serve God because we have yet to obtain a sterling education, the house of our dreams, abundant resources in the bank, super health or prime status at work, we will stay paralyzed or unproductive at best! We'll exist but we'll rarely feel alive!

God is not interested in our accomplishments or accumulations! He simply wants our faithfulness. In Psalm 51 King David finally begins to realize this:

"You do not delight in sacrifice or I would bring it; you do not take pleasure in burnt offerings. The sacrifices of God are a broken spirit; a broken and contrite heart, O God, you will not despise."

Security in Our Personal Lives

Some of you reading this book may be waiting for the *someday* of resolution of personal and emotional struggles. You are convinced that if only your individual circumstances or surroundings would change then your other issues would go away.

Perhaps you're a wife serving time in the prison of a disastrous marriage, longing for special intervention to unlock a door to relational freedom. Or you long for a new house, a job promotion, extra income or graduation from community college. *"I'm sure our relationship will improve one day – things will get better, I just know it,"* you fantasize.

You are confident that your marital difficulties are the fruit of your unmet securities. But instead of facing the hurts, disappointments and struggles of your relationship and choosing to address them head on, you have been infected by the *Someday Syndrome.* You've slipped into the coma of un-involvement and pretending. You continue to exist and breathe, but without moving ahead.

Unfortunately, more stuff or better looks doesn't change people on the inside. Poor marriages without much money will still be poor marriages with money. An unhappy wife without her college degree is an unhappy wife with one.

But when you and I firmly grasp our security in Christ, we are free to trust God to change us *NOW,* just as we are, in spite of our inadequacies, failures, and lousy situations. We can still make a difference in our world, marriage, job or even ministry if we see our value in Christ and nowhere else.

Facing Our Selfishness

If we're honest though, we must concede that waiting for our securities before we significantly change is basically sinful, doing things our way, not God's. In reality, we don't have faith that God is enough. In our minds we believe we must add something to God's love before He can work in us and through us.

Perhaps Jeremiah says it best of all when he speaks for God concerning Israel's continual refusal to obey God:

"This is what the Lord says: Let not the wise man boast of his wisdom or the strong man boast of his strength or the rich man boast of his riches. But let him who boasts boast about this: that he understands and knows me; that I am the Lord, who exercises

*kindness, justice and righteousness on earth, for in these I delight."
(Jeremiah 9: 23, 24)*

If we know God, we can live securely. There is nothing that should stop us from serving Him or from making significant changes in our lives. Listen to these passages from the Bible and the message of hope and security they offer:

"What then shall we say in response to this? If God is for us, who can be against us? Who shall separate us from the love of Christ? Shall trouble or hardship or persecution or famine or nakedness or danger or sword? (Romans 8: 31, 35ff)"

"My sheep listen to my voice; I know them, and they follow me. I give them eternal life, and they shall never perish; no one can snatch them out of my hand." (John 10: 27, 28)

"I have set the Lord always before me. Because he is at my right hand I will not be shaken. Therefore, my heart is glad and my tongue rejoices: my body also will rest secure." (Psalm 16: 8, 9)

What are you waiting for? A different job, more money, a new car, better looks? Another house, fancier clothes, a degree from high school or college? As long-time seminary prof, the late Howard Hendricks, once wrote, *"Action fulfills and strengthens knowledge and feeling. Consequently, it's a mistake to delay ministering to others till 'someday' when I'm ready to serve the Lord."*

God wants to change you and to use your life NOW! He longs to begin bearing fruit in you today, this week, this month. You may have been missing out on blessings like you have never known, all because you have been waiting for securities that you won't get and will never fulfill anyway.

In his classic book, *You Gotta Keep Dancin'*, climber Tim Hansel wisely states, *"When we give up our excessive need for security and 'clean victories,' for everything to be right, then the peace that passes all understanding has room to invade our lives again."*

Before moving on, let me suggest you take a moment or two and answer the questions at the end of this chapter. Be honest, but also anticipate what could happen

NOW! Discuss them with someone else, your spouse, a friend, a counselor, a pastor, small group, and contemplate what opportunities for change or service opportunities your security attachments have kept you from lately.

Ask God to help you let go of your demands which require that life be a nice, neat package complete with a money-back guarantee. Invite God to help you develop a new perspective on your body and material possessions, one that frees you to start NOW living a vibrant, world-changing life that gets better every year.

Once you have seriously considered your security quotient, move on to the next chapter where we will look at a second group of *somedays* that can also paralyze: RESPONSIBILITIES.

Things To Think About in Chapter 1

Read the story of the Prodigal Son in Luke 15: 11ff. What were the securities he thought would bring him happiness and fulfillment? What were the results of his seeking to find security his own way?

How does our society encourage and tempt us to go after temporal, earthly securities? Where should the Christian draw the line between being practically wise and trusting God for the results?

When have you felt most secure in your life? How old were you and how did you feel at the time? At what age do you suspect you will feel most secure about the future? Why?

Think of a security you have hung on to that left you unfulfilled? Why? What were the circumstances?

SOMEDAY AND RESPONSIBILITY
CHAPTER 2

"No one makes you feel inferior without your permission."
Eleanor Roosevelt

Lynn was an attractive 26-year-old woman who came to see me for counseling some years ago. Always tastefully dressed, stunningly manicured and brimming with success, Lynn effused an outward competence that was immediately engaging.

Inwardly, however, Lynn was a swirling pool of anguish and worry. Every day was driven by an overwhelming urgency to perform. No task for her could ever be totally completed, few relationships were fulfilling and her days never ended in satisfaction.

Given a job to do at church, Lynn would meticulously arrange the details, be careful to dot every "I" and cross every "t", only to rearrange the sub-tasks another time. Scores of extra phone calls, double-checks, and follow-ups preceded and followed every step of the process.

If Lynn were to plan a special event, she rarely enjoyed any of the process as it unfolded, but fretted over each detail like a neurosurgeon operating on a delicate aneurysm.

Lynn rarely felt she had ever done enough at her job, relationship or ministry. Although it was hard to admit, Lynn was terrified at the thought of letting someone down, failing or not having life neatly in control. If she were an airline pilot, she would no doubt safely and expertly guide the aircraft to a perfect landing, but would rarely see the magnificent views from 35,000 feet.

Only through many months of self-examination, soul-searching and deep, honest scrutiny of her past, did Lynn begin to relax her relentless urge to be overly responsible. In reality, she had to admit that her obsession about the details of life had paralyzed her from finding joy in her successes.

Paralyzed by Responsibility

Traits of hyper-responsibility seemed to be evident in the second character Jesus addresses in Luke 9. He, too, had an excuse as to why he couldn't follow Jesus, but his reasoning had a much different tone and motive from the first person. This follower seemed to have a legitimate, emotional request of Jesus, *"Permit me first to go and bury my Father."*

On the surface, this friend appeared to be saying something like, *"Lord, I've experienced a major tragedy in my family. Certainly, you understand that I need to be there with my loved ones and help with the arrangements!"*

But Jesus, in what must have seemed to the man like a rather uncaring response, replied, *"Allow the dead to bury their own dead; but as for you go and proclaim everywhere the kingdom of God."* (v. 60) Could Jesus be so insensitive as to place His own immediate ministry above his care for this man grieving the loss of his father?

Thankfully, if when you consider the culture of the day, that wasn't the case at all. Instead, Jesus was performing an MRI on this man's excuse only to reveal another *someday* driven response.

Children from Jewish families were expected to care for their parents right up to the time of their father's or mother's death. There was a special bond between parents and children in the Jewish extended family and a sense of responsibility that unfortunately has been lost in much of our culture today.

The truth is that the man's father had not recently passed on as we might think. No, instead of a grieving man talking to Jesus, we have here an individual caught up in the responsibilities of family life. It is more likely that Jesus' second would-be follower was postponing service for God until his responsibilities at home were completed. And that obligation, the burial of his father, was likely a long way off!

It's possible that this man was not excusing himself for a few days or weeks, but rather for many, many years!

Home, Sweet Home

If you are a homeowner you realize as I do that there is always something you could be doing to maintain or improve your house. I remember the time when we had just moved into a new home in Illinois. It was a very exciting opportunity for us to say the least. As a pastor, however, myriad duties took over calling for my attention during every unrestricted moment I had.

There was a lawn to seed, shrubs to plant, landscaping to design, walls to paint and boxes to move - the list seemed endless! I recall one afternoon returning home from the office and sensing an almost magnetic tug to diminish that long list a notch or two.

As I began to change into my work clothes, I suddenly stopped in my tracks. Perhaps through the Holy Spirit's initiation, I said to my wife Jackie, "*You know, it would be possible to stay so busy working on this house that we would rarely take the time to enjoy it!*"

At that very moment I poured myself a cup of coffee, made my way to the deck located just off our kitchen, sat down in our porch swing and stared out at the beautiful woods that sprawled behind our home.

All around me was a lawn of dirt and weeds.

However, for a few uninterrupted minutes I didn't care. It was incredibly refreshing to be still for a moment or two and stop to enjoy what God had given us NOW.

You see, there is always something else to accomplish, begging, seducing, calling us to give it our immediate attention. The culture tells us every day that busier is better, doing more is healthier. It's rare to see a commercial for products that actually slow our pace down and give us more time to rest.

And home is only one of myriad responsibilities demanding our attention. You can no doubt think of commitments unique to you that require your attention every day. Let's take a look at several common ones for most individuals and families.

The Workplace

Responsibilities can reign over us at our place of employment, too. And often what doesn't get perfected at the office gets taken home. Computers, e-mails, texts and cell phones seductively beckon us to attend to them no matter where we are. Add that two-thirds of the homes in America have two parents working and the responsibility merry-go-round is spinning out of control in most families!

Bosses demand more of our time, so that more products will be sold, so that more money will be made, so that more profits will be gained. Since jobs are often scarce, middle-agers wonder if they are marketable any more. The world seems so competitive these days and people drive themselves trying to cover every base in the office or online so they can stay in the rat race just a little bit longer.

Thirty years ago, it was predicted that we would only work thirty-hour weeks. Today the normative reality is closer to 50 or more and the workplace now includes much more time at home as our work culture evolves and now as a world-wide pandemic continues to impact us in ways we never imagined.

The Church

Church growth surveys have shown for years that typically eighty percent of the work in most churches is accomplished by twenty percent of the people. Obviously, many Christians in ministry are overworked and facing burnout! Pastors are often overwhelmed by how much there is to do. In fact, more and more are quitting the ministry or flaming out.

Thankfully, some churches are catching the vision of utilizing the multitude of gifts and talents in their entire congregations, seeing a substantial growth in the percentage of people actively involved in ministry.

Nevertheless, the busy-ness of most church calendars still sucks many people into over-activity and responsibility while using guilt to get more out of those already too busy.

Jesus knew that our man in Luke 9, enslaved by the daily requirements of life, could stumble on the rocks of pending responsibility if he endeavored to follow the Teacher. He would be like the toddler holding his mom's hand but tripping over his own feet because he wants to peer into each and every store window that they pass.

Likewise, many of us continually peer into the windows of responsibilities that pull at us from so many directions. Following Jesus may necessitate that some loose ends do not get tied up. Some clients will not get called back, certain activities won't take place and a few goals are never reached. Our homes may not always be spotless, projects won't always get completed, we may have to say "NO" now and then.

Yes, some church ministries may even have to wait for a while. Am I advocating laziness and irresponsibility? As Paul often said, "*May it never be.*" Other scripture will not allow us that freedom and Jesus spoke against purely slothful behavior.

Don't forget Paul's reminders that we should *"do our work heartily, as to the Lord,"* (Colossians 3:21) and to, *"Be careful how you walk, not as unwise men, but as wise, making the most of your time, because the days are evil."* (Ephesians 5: 15, 16)

Using our time and resources efficiently and capably is a cornerstone of wise and productive living and ministry. However, the *Someday Syndrome* victim typically allows too much responsibility to become a mountain that he or she cannot climb, and as a result becomes disabled part way through the ascent and goes nowhere.

Or she doesn't grow and get any better. She becomes stymied by fatigue from overwork and debilitated by the despair she feels when the mountain of work never appears to dissipate.

What responsibilities are keeping you from moving intentionally forward in your life walk? Are you a parent waiting for your child to get into school first before you do anything else God is asking? Of course, our children do require more attention in those early years and parents need to be there to love them, care for them and enjoy the special moments of their growing up years.

But too many moms with young children have resolved to sit on the shelf of motherhood, allowing their personal and spiritual growth to stagnate in a pool of exhaustion and guilt.

Many parents of the 21st Century feel the *responsibility* to see that their children are involved in every possible activity available at the school, community or church, driving themselves to the brink of exhaustion while grasping their badge of courage going to three games and four meetings in one week!

Perhaps you are part of a mid-life couple, biding your time until the clock strikes RETIREMENT. *"We've got to get our affairs in order,"* you say, and you permit the ticking of your biological watch to march on while you wait for better days on Social Security.

Are you the dedicated worker who would love to quit his job, move on to something far more enriching and fulfilling but cannot because, "*they need me there right now?*" Somehow, you've been wooed into believing that your company or business will fall apart if you relinquish your key role there.

Taking the Plunge

A number of years ago I found myself in a full-time position where I had happily served for 14 years. The people I worked with were generally wonderful, my bosses were my friends, I knew year after year what my tasks were and people told me often that I had performed admirably.

But during my last two or three years something seemed profoundly wrong. My gifts and my talents were not being utilized and I began to function more as a robot than as a rich contributor to the ministry. As I began to reflect on the possibility of leaving, however, my musings threatened to disable me. My energy and enthusiasm were gone.

Nevertheless, I began to say to myself, "*But look at all the things I'm doing here. Won't I be letting people down if I go? This place and its people have taught me volumes over the years. Can I just walk away from it all? Besides, it's so comfortable here. If I go, I can never come back in the same capacity. What about my family? What if I make a terrible mistake.*"?

As I look back now, I tremble thinking that I might have remained where I had no business being anymore because I was unwilling to risk appearing irresponsible. And interestingly enough, had I stayed, no one would have known I had made a mistake but me!

I could have continued to live outwardly gratified, but internally ravaged by discontent and misery.

Is there a tug at your heart right now to be doing something more significant for God? Are you caught in the trap of activity burnout, feeling impotent to alter your life trajectory, much less influence the life of another?

It is likely that you will have to start by making basic changes in your life, moving forward and risking opportunities, to assure yourself that your responsibilities shouldn't keep you from a major change or significant growth. You may need to say, "no," and actually experience the world holding together after you said it!

The Joy of Bath Therapy

At one point in my counseling with Lynn, the client I spoke of earlier, I proposed that she consider trying *bath therapy*. Actually, I had no knowledge of any such program. I made it up.

But I believed Lynn needed to attempt a radically new way of living, even if it was only in something small. So, I urged Lynn, especially when she began to feel overwhelmed that evening from the *weight* of all she had to do, to try something radical for her.

I urged to fill her bathtub up with hot water and bubbles, place some magazines or a good book nearby and thoroughly soak for one hour. She could add more hot water as needed. I admit that I have done that now and then and found it wonderfully refreshing.

I wish, however, that I could report that Lynn was thrilled with my idea. Instead she was furious with me! She argued that taking a bath was just some stupid psychological trick and she couldn't see what it had to do with her problems. She believed that to solve her struggles with responsibility she must do it "responsibly!"

In fact, Lynn is typical of those who are obsessively careful about meeting everyone's expectations and who finally seek help. They do the same thing in their counseling - they always want to perform by the book and then some. Every week they come back to the counselor, making sure they have finished everything they are supposed to do.

They take copious notes and follow every assignment to a tee.

They would love their counselor, pastor or helper to give them a list of things to do each week to get better and they would do them perfectly! This group of *Someday Syndromers* are typically advice-seekers and demand *answers*, not things to think about or ponder.

I've learned over the years to respond a bit differently when I sense I am talking with someone like this. Usually they mention several alternatives that they are trying to decide on and will then pause, waiting for me to tell them what to do.

My usual response is something like, *"Well, John, I'll be interested to see which one of those options you decide on."*

At that point I usually receive an incredibly disappointed and shocked expression, one of betrayal and rejection. And yet I have discovered that in the end they can learn to make decisions on their own, even when the result is not guaranteed.

Thankfully, months after our bath discussion, Lynn told me that she was *still taking those baths.* She had begun to discover, in a silly, small way, that she could never do enough or be enough in any task, effort or job and that was OK with God. The world would still be spinning even though she had made a choice not to keep trying.

She began to acquire a new-found sense of release from the demands she had thrust on herself years ago to always come through for others no matter what the price.

Lynn continued a life of chosen actions in lieu of her formally compulsive ones, choosing now to be less obsessive about all she had to do and accomplish. She had started to live fundamentally different.

We're Not In the Trinity

Many like Lynn believe that the affairs and outcomes of the entire world sit on their shoulders. When they say *no* to someone's request for assistance, they try to find someone else to do it. When a request for help comes calling from church or work or the community, they are determined to somehow meet the need if they can't.

I remember being asked to be the Master of Ceremonies for a banquet at a church I used to attend. I responded to the man making the request that I didn't have anything that evening but wanted to spend time at home with my family.

I sensed that he didn't understand my negative response so to avoid conflict I began to try and find him a substitute MC! I took on a responsibility that I had no reason to claim as my own.

If we're honest, we must admit that our taking responsibility for others' actions and responses is ungodly at best. Most people are familiar with the common (and true) description of the Godhead: *God the Father, God the Son, God the Holy Spirit.* But some of us might better say it concerning us like this: *God, the Father, God the Son, God, the Holy Spirit and ME!*

We need to let God deal with how people act, respond, think and feel. We can help but we're not in charge of all that. Daniel 4:35 reminds us of God's sovereignty and control: *"And all the inhabitants of the earth are accounted as nothing, But He does according to His will in the host of heaven and among the inhabitants of the earth; And no one can ward off His hand or say to Him, 'What have you done?'"*

Few, of course, would question that good deeds are essential for Christian living. Sometimes we must go the extra mile. The book of Titus in fact says, *"In all things show yourself to be an example of good deeds. . . to be ready for every good deed . . . to let our people also learn to engage in good deeds to meet pressing needs." (2:7; 3:1; 3:14)*

In contrast, however, Paul also explains to Titus that the groundwork for living, our salvation in Christ, is

NOT based on those same good works. *"He saved us, not on the basis of deeds which we have done in righteousness, but according to His mercy."*

We can never do enough to earn our salvation nor our ultimate worth in this world.

As a result, we can better understand Jesus' seemingly caustic remark to the disciple in Luke 9, and see the underlying motives Jesus was attempting to expose. This man would never be ready to fully serve Christ as long as the responsibilities of life still controlled him.

Only when he was ready to surrender as Mary did and declare, *"Be it done to me according to your word,"* would he be ready for commitment as a follower of Jesus. What so-called *responsibilities* are restricting you from moving more and more toward Christ-like character?

What self-inflicted demands have doused the fire you used to have in you to serve others?

Getting your kids into school? Making enough money at your second job to just get over the hump? adopting as your own every task that pleads for help, spiritual or not? Waiting until your parents are "settled in their retirement? Finishing your education? Paying off all your debts? Making your kid a star?

Seeing your teen graduate from high school? Fulfilling your obligation to the many church teams you serve?

As noble as any of these milestones might be, they are all grossly deficient to satisfy us. There will always be another major obligation seductively beckoning us to perform.

You can be assured that Satan will do all he can to keep every believer from growing. He would love us to get so caught up in taking care of everyday business that we God's plan all together. It is a lie from the pit of Hell that we must have life all together and every commitment fulfilled before we can be of use to God.

If that were true then the Apostle Paul, John Mark, David, Moses and myriad other Bible characters would have never made it onto God's honor roll.

Paul's challenge in Colossians 3 now takes on even more striking importance. *"If then you have been raised up with Christ, keep seeking the things above, where Christ is seated at the right hand of God. Set your mind on things above, not on the things that are on the earth."* (vv. 1,2)

We all know those who are so heavenly minded that they are no earthly good, but that's not who Paul is addressing here. Notice the progressive tense of the words, "keep seeking." An ongoing commitment is what it will take to serve God completely. We must look to God for His perspective on life so that we do not don't get trapped by demands that we think are so important.

Remember Martha, Mary's sister, who got so wrapped up in trying to prepare food for Jesus that she almost missed experiencing Jesus? (Luke 10:38-42) Jesus' words at the time expressed the same cautions as those in Luke 9 when he rebuked her; *"Martha, Martha, you are worried and bothered about so many things; But only a few things are necessary, really only one, for Mary has chosen the good part, which shall not be taken away from her."*

If you are stuck in freeway traffic in any major city in America, you can usually tune your car radio to the traffic copter zooming through the skies above you. As you listen, the reporter tells you the cause of your predicament and roughly how long it will take you to get to your destination.

Although this heavenly view does not deliver you from the log jam of automobiles, it does give you *perspective* you need to not allow this present slow down to ruin your day. God's view also keeps our responsibilities in the proper view.

Notice Paul's reminder in Ephesians 5, *"Be careful how you walk, not as unwise men, but as wise, making the most of your time because the days are evil."* And yet, too often the demands of life control us rather than us controlling them.

Is your typical day something like this? Waking the kids up in the morning, getting dressed, fixing breakfast for the family, going off to work or getting your spouse there, attending to 3 school activities and one for church, stopping by the doctor's office, picking up the kids, taking them back to wherever they came from later, attending church or a meeting that night and plopping exhausted into bed after the kids are asleep?

If you are a teen or college student, your day may be even more saturated with activities from school to clubs to church to work with barely a moment free for yourself. If a compulsion to simply be more responsible is the source, check your pulse for *someday syndrome* symptoms.

The *Gods* revisited?

In the Old Testament a constant but chosen thorn in the flesh for Israel was allowing false gods in its kingdoms. One king would tear them down but the next king would permit the newer images to stay. Even Solomon, the wisest of all rulers, *"went after Ashtoreth the goddess of the Sidonians and after Milcom the detestable idol of the Ammonites."* (I Kings 11:5)

I can't help but believe that busyness and the pursuit of what people often call *responsibilities* - sports involvement, special classes, lessons, pressures galore - are the new idols being worshipped by many today. Time for faith-building, ministry, Sabbath rest, productive change and healthy growth have been driven onto the altar of activity, sacrificing the prominence of God's kingdom in the process.

Time for family, relaxation, reading for pleasure and just enjoying our homes, our kids, and even our possessions is becoming extinct in America today. No wonder so few today are able to, *"Be still and know that I am God."* (Psalm 46:10)

Is it any surprise that healthy families are becoming rare and dysfunctional households are more the norm?

Millions claim in various polls that they have a relationship with God and yet few know the God of the universe intimately. And yet both testaments of scripture exhort us to make knowing God, not knowing about Him or merely doing godly things, the crux of our faith.

Remember again Jeremiah 9:23, 24, *"Thus says the Lord, 'Let not a wise man boast of his wisdom, and let not the mighty man boast of his might, let not a rich man boast of his riches; but let him who boasts boast of this, that he understands and knows Me, that I am the Lord who exercises lovingkindness, justice and righteousness on earth; for I delight in these things,' declares the Lord. "*

Paul urges us in a similar fashion: *"That I may know Him, and the power of His resurrection and the fellowship of His sufferings, being conformed to His death . . . . '"* Philippians 3: 10

Should we be amazed that fewer and fewer Christians are students of the Bible, forsaking the opportunity to build a rock-solid foundation upon which to live a productive, rich, contemplative life in Christ?

Sometimes I long for the simple days of Jesus' time when people were forced to spend long hours each day traveling from place to place. The moments of solitude they enjoyed to meditate, question, and re-think all they had learned must have helped to sink Jesus' life-changing words deep into their souls. Responsibilities were far more limiting and one could concentrate on the major tasks of the day.

I have often envied a good friend of mine who is a truck driver because of the *quiet* times he has every day for hours on end. No one to talk to, no one's needs to be met . . .just the wide-open road.

We have little opportunity any more to do what Mary did when she *treasured all these things in her heart.* Christians rarely ponder things these days. Our worships services often lack time and space to simply enjoy God, while sitting, standing or singing in His presence, again offering our body, soul and spirit above all to Him.

The Choice

None of us is immune from the draining pull of responsibility. On the other hand, we all still retain our ability to choose how we will live. It would help if you would take a moment or two and list below those *responsibilities* that dominate your life right now. Some of them probably cannot be altered very much. Others, however, could be eliminated or at least reduced in time and demand.

We must be willing to say *no*. We must be prepared to look at the big picture and ask ourselves, *What am I accomplishing by doing all these things? Do I think I am personally responsible for how everything turns out at work or at church or in my community?*

For many, over-activity is a place to not have to face the difficult circumstances that have crept into their world. And unfortunately, overwork and zealousness appear acceptable to those who are watching. *What a servant's heart she has! Wow, Mel will just do anything for you, won't he? Is Pastor Tom a go-getter or what? We got a gem when we got him!* are often accolades given to the ultra-responsible.

And yet behind all the good works may be an aching heart seeking for love and acceptance in all the wrong places. I'll discuss this idea in more detail in chapters four and five on *Fear* and *Fantasy.*

Questions Worth Asking

Are you running from what you know God is asking you to consider? Are you, like the second individual in Luke 9, giving God a shallow excuse for why you cannot become all that He wants you to be NOW? Do you need to be changing a habit, attitude or behavior but instead are waiting in the purgatory of responsibility for the world to change first?

For now, as you ponder your list, ask God what He might be asking you to do instead. Perhaps He wants you to spend more time with your family, to become a better student of the Bible, to work at changing some debilitating habits or reactions you possess, to begin to minister to people in your neighborhood. Perhaps he wants you to QUIT certain activities and slow down, get to know Him better, not just know about Him.

God wants our faithfulness far more than our busyness. Psalm 54:6 says, *"Willingly I will sacrifice to Thee; I will give thanks to Thy name, O Lord, for it good."*

Do you want to serve Jesus? Do you need to change? Are you tired of the prison of unnecessary demands? It's time to LET GO of all that! Admit you have been sinful by somehow thinking you could do enough to make life work.

Admit the selfishness of avoiding God's desired changes for you, whether personal or ministry related, and ask God to forgive you and to help you begin to take the first steps toward significant change.

Next, we move on to chapter 3 where will talk about a third set of *somedays* - RELATIONSHIPS.

Things to Think About in Chapter 2

What current responsibilities do I believe must be done before I can move on with other important things?

Who in my life may have modeled the over-responsibility urge that I model NOW?

What else could I be doing NOW that would be pleasing to me and to God if I didn't have all these other demands on my time.

SOMEDAY AND RELATIONSHIPS
CHAPTER 3

"We all want our lives to work well, to become better than they are or to remain as good as they are." Larry Crabb

Several years before my wife Jackie and I were married, she was engaged to someone else. The date was set, tentative arrangements had been made and everything seemed right except for one minor concern. Jackie was miserable. She was keenly aware that the flame of love for her fiancé was no longer burning. In fact, it may have never been ignited at all, with only smoldering ashes of genuine attraction remaining in her heart.

She had to get out. But what would people say? His parents, her parents, friends, other family members? Being in her mid-twenties, she wondered if this was her last chance to reach the altar. Would singleness be her lot in life and her tombstone one day (at least in her mind) read, *"Here Lies One Solitary Life?"*

Although it was perhaps the toughest decision she ever made, Jackie called off her engagement, crying for days afterwards, confused, often questioning her decision during the subsequent painful weeks. *"Could this misery be part of God's will?"* she often wondered during especially dark moments.

The inertia of marriage planning had subsided and Jackie found herself in a straightjacket of confusion, discouragement and despondency. Hopes for an intimate, caring and life-long relationship had now dissipated into an empty loneliness. The anticipation of a blissful, married life to someone she couldn't live without became a dream she must in her mind do without.

The Reality of Broken Hearts

Most people at some point undergo the pain of a broken or hurting relationship. Childhood arguments, lost teenage loves, severed engagements, distant spouses, friendship splits, divorces, sudden deaths, abuse, rejections by parents. The list is usually long.

All of us, nevertheless, crave for someone to love us unconditionally and accept us for who we are, in spite of our deficiencies, lack of good looks or social standing. God designed us to long for Him and attempts to find perfect love elsewhere only leaves us wanting for more. Let's go back to *Psalm 42:1,2: "As the deer pants for streams of water, so my soul pants for You, O God. My soul thirsts for God, for the living God . . ."*

Psalm 63 echoes the same message and imagery: "O God, You are my God; earnestly I seek you: My soul thirsts for you, my body longs for you, in a dry and weary land where there is no water."

Thirsting hearts! It's our parched souls longing for love that fuels our craving for relationship that works, fulfills, and never lets us down. Our souls hunger and thirst for more but our core is empty. Much like homeless beggars, we desperately hang on to any crumb of compassion or significance thrown our way, hoping it might satisfy our empty emotional cavities even if only for a while.

Sadly, however, the pain from past relational hurts has seduced us into wandering perilously apart from God, the One who could provide our satisfaction that we desired in human relationships.

Gary Sinclair

Yes, intimacy can be wonderful. God ordained
marriage as a sacred and wondrous union of two people
in body, soul and spirit. The love between a parent and
child may be one of the most incredible bonds imaginable
in the human matrix.

Jesus' familiar statement in John 15:13, *"Greater love has
no one than this, that one lay down his life for his friends,"* is a
poignant example of the potential richness of personal
affection.

But other people will never be enough to satisfy our
souls. (I'll say more about this in chapters four and five).
Therefore, it is no surprise that the third and final
someday of Luke 9 involves a potential follower's struggle
with RELATIONSHIP.

During this concluding scenario, a third disciple
approaches Jesus to assure Him of his devotion to the
Christ. *"I will follow you, Lord,"* he said, *"but first let me go
back and say goodbye to my family."* (v. 61)

Jesus, in his unremitting straightforwardness, replies,
*"No one, after putting his hand to the plow and looking back, is fit
for the kingdom of God."* Once again there seems to be an
uncharacteristic callousness in Jesus, the Teacher, as this
third man seemed to want to merely kiss mom and dad
goodbye and express his love to his friends before
departing with Jesus.

Of course, if greeting family were the only issue, Jesus
probably would have allowed this man to return to them
and say their goodbyes.

However, notice Jesus' analogy in His response. He
specifically uses a word picture from farming, an
appropriate example since many of Jesus' followers and
hearers were familiar with agricultural settings. He states
that, *"No one after putting his hand to the plow, and looking back,
(italics mine), is fit for the kingdom of God."*

Like the previous two examples, this brother intended
more than he was indicating in his reply. He had an
intention that was more than a heartfelt goodbye. Jesus

44

discerned a deeper motive for the man's reluctance to follow him.

Most likely this individual feared that following Christ might actually terminate or impede meaningful and life-giving relationship with those to whom he was closest, perhaps with his mother and father, maybe a wife or future spouse or possibly his dearest of friends. He knew this man was capable as we all are of substituting human relationship for God as our ultimate source of intimacy.

Dr. Larry Crabb, in his now classic book, *Inside Out*, speaks at length about man's longing or thirst for relationship and states the following:

"I was designed for relationship. I want someone to be involved with me who is strong enough to handle everything about me without retreating or feeling threatened."

But only God is capable of perfectly meeting such a need. The words of David in Psalm 63 continue: *"Because your lovingkindness is better than life, my lips will glorify You . . . My soul will be satisfied as with the richest of foods." (v. 3)*

Unfortunately, our sinful tendencies entice us to pursue the quenching of our thirst through human interactions such as spouse with spouse, parent with child or friend with friend. We also begin to demand that every human relationship somehow work, to make us feel complete, worthwhile and fully loved.

We think we must be married, experience forgiveness from family members, be understood by our coworkers, always get a date, be told we are appreciated, get applause from our parents and all sorts of other things if we are to be okay.

Am I suggesting we shouldn't want or enjoy human relationship and success? Of course not. We were made for fellowship, to work together, to serve in complementary ways as part of Christ's body, the church.

We were designed to enjoy one another but not at the price of pushing Christ to second place. Our intimacy with Christ actually enhances and strengthen our closeness with the others in our lives.

Single Sadness

Nearly half of our adult population today is unmarried! And yet, without a doubt the so-called curse of singleness has caused one of the greatest defections from the ranks of those who serve Jesus.

Family members don't help either when they pester young adults with, *"Isn't it about time you found a nice girl (guy) to settle down with?"*

Consequently, millions of Christians, most notably those in their 20's and 30's, stay frozen in time while they wait for a spouse to come along. They repeatedly tell themselves, *"My problem is that I don't have a life partner yet. But someday I will and then I can do those other things people expect of me."*

Unfortunately, when a future spouse's presence is not imminent, singles often allow compulsive, demanding habits to dull the ache of being unmarried and take control. Is it any wonder that recent research shows that young adults are leaving our churches in droves? While there are additional reasons for their departure, the push to be married before they can play a significant role is a factor.

As a pastor and counselor for four decades or more, I've worked with lots of young adults. And many of them were battling one or more compulsive behaviors: pornography, overeating, workaholism, ministry overload, too much spending. Ironically, a good number were also full-time Christian workers like pastors, campus ministers, missionaries, associate staff to name a few.

Dr. Crabb again writes, *"Most habits that we seem powerless to control grow out of our attempts to relieve the unbearable tension that results from our failure to deal with the disappointment of our deepest longings for relationship."*

Many of my former clients came for assistance under the weight of overwhelming guilt and feeling powerlessness to change their world. Those involved in ministries found their efforts hollow, sensing they were going through the motions without any hint of God's blessing in their lives.

Their lack of a life's companion became a weight and distraction that kept them from being who they were at the moment. Doors of service and opportunities for change were there to be entered but marriage had become the key to their ultimate happiness!

Social life became their anesthetic to dull the pain of being helper-less. Without some sort of Novocain, the questions of, *"Am I really that unlovable?" "Does anyone want me?" "If people who I care about don't want me, then who does?"* remained unanswered and life uncomplete.

Singleness was an inconvenient, even irritating, layover on their flight through life to marital bliss, rather than a possible fulfilling part of God's ultimate plan

The pull of relationship seems even stronger among those who are *divorced*. They have already tasted marital oneness. They usually know what it is like to be loved, to be selected as the number one choice of another human being, to have been drawn into a family or group of people who deeply mattered to one another.

But when the relationship ends, a part of them seemingly dies. As one of my clients put it, *"I had this beautiful picture of how life was going to be lived out and now it's gone."* For this reason alone, divorce in our society is one of the greatest social tragedies of all time.

God hates divorce for a reason! (Malachi 2: 16) He understands the hurt and trauma that occurs when two people enmeshed as one are torn apart. He must sigh a heavenly sigh whenever He sees the confusion, turmoil and anguish of the children of divorced parents.

And yet, what do most divorced people and children of divorced parents do to find fulfillment? Demand another relationship or fight to get the first one back! Even if they were being mistreated, perhaps abused in the relationship, they will often battle to return.

The client I mentioned above is still utilizing much of her emotional energy being angry at her former husband for ruining her picture. She is stuck in the *someday* of having a relationship like the one she lost, believing that she'll never be full or complete until she has it.

The Curse of Abuse

Abuse is rampant in our society, isn't it? No one is immune either. Children, wives, secretaries, neighbors, employees are all likely candidates to suffer from some form of abuse. More and more seems to surface every year even in places we would never expect it such as the church!

And yet millions of people remain in abusive, destructive and potentially lethal home and family situations as they fantasize about how much better their relationships could be again one day. They rarely resist the perpetrator, choosing rather to clutch to the crumbs of relationship that remain.

But because the pull in us toward relationship is so pervasive, the abused are often still consumed with the fantasy of more involvement with those who abuse them. They so want to believe that the next time they're in contact things will be different.

"Today dad will notice my intelligence, tomorrow the boss will like my work, this trip home mom will be proud of me," they muse. *"He said he won't abuse me anymore. I know he won't."* (I'll speak more about this in chapter five.)

Therefore, to many in this heartbreaking category involving people relationships, perhaps one that includes you, life becomes just another *someday*. We wait for marriage, hope for a restored relationship, demand someone see us as we really are or dream that others will change. And we once again postpone getting better while waiting for *someday* to come.

Why? Because we all thirst for intimacy with others as though our lives depended on it. (See chapter 12) We don't believe that life could possibly be enough with these people connections established in our world in some way.

Relationship through our children

I can't help but think of the thousands of missionaries over the years who've had to make one of the greatest relational sacrifices of all, time with their kids. Many of these saints of God have graciously accepted the call of God to lands where the only alternative is to send their dearest possessions, from grade school to high school age, off to boarding school for 8 to 10 months of the year.

Yes, email and the online connecting have made communication so much easier today but the cost is still huge.

When I was in college, I had an opportunity to serve for the summer with a missionary family, the Netlands, in Aomori, Japan. Not long after I arrived, we went down to the boat docks to wait for the arrival of the ferry that would bring their children home from school for the summer.

I'll never forget watching Mr. Netland nervously, yet full of excitement, peer into the darkness, straining to see the first sign of the huge ship that was bringing his children home. Soon the boat docked and as the little ones bolted down that walkway, they were engulfed by Mr. Netland's huge loving arms, tears of joy trickling down his cheeks.

Even as I write about that experience from decades ago, I tears are welling up in my own eyes as I think about my grown kids who are out of the house now. It has never been quite the same as it was when we were all together.

We find ourselves now valuing family time more than ever. Yes, if we want to serve Jesus our relationships may require separation, strain, unfulfillment, and loss.

"How could you leave your children even to serve God?" a friend might ask. We will have to look forward, not behind, with our eyes on Jesus if we are ever to make such a sacrifice. Sometimes I wish these verses from Matthew 10:37-39 weren't in the Scriptures::

"Anyone who loves his father or mother more than me is not worthy of me; anyone who loves his son or daughter more than me is not worthy of me; and anyone who does not take his cross and follow me is not worthy of me. Whoever finds his life will lose it, and whoever loses his life for my sake will find it."

However, we can also expect too much of our children while they are still with us. A number of years ago my family and I had the opportunity of watching Tim our son play in the championship game of his end-of-the-year freshman tournament in basketball. They won a very close game and we were certainly proud of Tim's performance!

It was wonderful to enjoy the moment of their victory, seeing them slapping each other on the backs and giving each other high fives, accepting the trophy that they so richly deserved. As parents the moments don't get much better than that!

And yet the day was soon over and life settled back into normalcy. The thrill of the boys' conquest was still very real, but the summit of emotion was gone. I realized again that relationship in this world is never totally fulfilling. The satisfaction of what our children give us doesn't last. As parents it is easy for us to somehow think that our kids are capable of soothing the aches of our inner beings and yet they don't and can't.

Although our children make us proud so often as Tim did that day, they also fail, are not always appreciative, don't necessarily respond to our loving actions and words, and make decisions with which we disagree or even violently oppose.

And yet many people look desperately, though subtly perhaps, to children to somehow provide them with the happiness and fulfillment they have never known.

"Someday," they scream inside, *"my son will make something out of his life." "My daughter will be successful. I'll see to it,"* another demands. And in the meantime, their own lives grind to a screeching halt, paralyzed by their quest for faulty relationship at best through their children.

Let me also speak to those of you who may be wanting children but for some reason can't conceive. The longing to bear a child, especially for a woman, is a passion that finds its roots deep within the soul.

Although we were fortunate to have our son, Tim, just as we had planned, our daughter Amy was born only after my wife's challenge with endometriosis. We faced the very real possibility that we would have no other children.

If you are waiting to have a child you too may contend with the *Someday Syndrome*, the pull within you to somehow postpone significant change, happiness and joy until some future time when a child enters your household. Don't sell you and your spouse short!

Ask God what He wants to do in your life while you are still childless! Make specific efforts to enjoy God, each other and the time He has given you NOW. Let Him strengthen your faith and point you more directly toward His purposes even in the middle of your sadness.

Mending fences with parents

Jack is a recovering alcoholic. He hasn't had a drink for over six years now. And yet his adult life, even subsequent to his sobriety, has incurred a failed marriage, loss of a business, a string of huge debts, periodic bouts with the law, strained relations with his family members and a trail of mistrust with most everyone who really gets to know him.

Jack is a pleaser though. To be around him is to feel like you have known him for years. He promises things to everybody. *"I'll have that check to you on Friday," "Sure, I can stop by and fix that tomorrow." "Yeah, I plan on being at church this week. You can count on it," "No problem, I'll be able to attend the game, Bill."*

I had known about Jack's way of life for quite a while and had spent a lot of time with him, trying to help him sort out why he was the way he was. I'll never forget one day when we were talking and he told me about how his real father, who he still has contact with now and then, had left him when he was four years old.

At one point in the conversation I said to him, *"Jack, you really feel abandoned by your dad, don't you?"* It was at that point that Jack began sobbing uncontrollably for the next several minutes. The word *abandon* stirred something powerful and painful deep within.

From that point on we began to explore how Jack has spent much of his life trying to hang on to every shred of relationship he could by never letting anyone down, always promising he could come through for others or smothering them with his demand that they never leave him.

Unfortunately, no one could keep all the promises Jack made and so others simply didn't trust him anymore. For a while, alcohol served as an anesthetic for the pain of his lost loves. Jack was determined he would never be left alone again.

Faced with the possibility of losing visitation rights to his son, he gave up alcohol but found more painkiller in pleasing everyone and spending a lot of money. He often went to visit his dad, hoping that somehow his father would finally be proud of him, see some worth in him, tell him he was doing well, but dad was always more interested in his own life than Jack's.

NOW!

To this day, as far as I know, Jack is waiting for someday when everything is going to come together and he will show dad and others that he really is somebody. You can hear it in his voice, *"Soon I'm going to get close again to the Lord. But first . . . "*

Unfortunately, Jack lives in a fantasy world of thinking he will get married soon and I understand has even started drinking again. How sad.

Not looking back

All this brings us to Jesus' response to our third friend in Luke 9, *"No one, after putting his hand to the plow and looking back, is fit for the kingdom of God."*

In central Illinois where we lived for seventeen years, farmland is plentiful to say the least. I've joked now and then that it was so flat there I could see Denver from my back porch! Even though I grew up a city kid, I did learn a little bit about farming during those years in the middle of corn and soybeans.

In fact, when we first moved there one of the farmers showed me how to fill my own turkey for Thanksgiving!

And while I'll never be a farmer or even think like one, I did discover one basic rule that is included in every farmer's unwritten handbook, a principle which Jesus undoubtedly understood as he spoke.

When a field is plowed the first pass through must be straight.

If the first row isn't straight the others won't be either. Of course, today the farmer uses machinery worth hundreds of thousands of dollars guided by a GPS system to make his task of alignment that much easier.

One of our other farmers actually let me drive his combine to harvest some soybeans and believe me, even with all the bells and whistles, it was like piloting the *Queen Mary*! But just imagine, in Jesus' day there was at most only a work animal pulling a one-row plow.

The farmer can't remove his eyes from the guide point or his first row would be crooked and as a consequence all the other rows would be out of line as well. To look back, to be distracted, to set off without resolve to complete the project would never result in a bountiful harvest.

Jesus responded bluntly that the kingdom of God would require no less. A follower of Christ cannot chronically peer over his shoulder at past personal involvements, lousy relationships or childhood traumas, as devastating or as unfulfilling as they might have been. Neither can a woman of God continue to be distracted by her longing to be married or to have children, as wonderful as a spouse, a beautiful wedding and parenting can be.

Jesus knew that not only will earthly relationships never totally satisfy us, but many components of our relationships are out of our control anyway. The spouse who won't change, the guy who won't get serious with a woman, the father who can't admit his abusive behavior, the son who will not obey his parents have all chosen to act the way they do.

We can desire that someone change and fervently pray for their transformation. We can counsel them, listen well, communicate our ideas and provide an atmosphere conducive to change, but they may still choose otherwise.

You see, demanding that others change is a form of looking back over our shoulder. When our lives stagnate because of what others choose to do or not do, we limit our potential to grow into the person God intended for us to be and any fruit from our personal harvest is likely to be meager at best.

But let me return to our journey because there's much more to our tale and a lot of it's good!

The Rest of the Story

Not too long after Jackie called off her engagement, God spoke to her quite clearly (though not audibly) about her situation. He challenged her to live in the present, ministering with the gifts and talents she had right then and not to wait until she was married. God also told her that she was not a second-class citizen because of her singleness.

She began to invite people, most of them married, over to her apartment for meals, choosing not to run from the hurt she felt by not being married. Instead she began to purposefully and meaningfully reach out to others in spite of her present circumstances.

God wonderfully blessed her efforts and gave her a sense of purpose and distinction, knowing that, at least for the time being, she could minister to others while still learning and becoming whole in the process.

As you might guess there was a happy ending to this story when I came along and the rest as they say is history!

However, the crucial result is not Jackie's ultimate marriage. Others might endure the same initial circumstances and end up not ever marrying. The most powerful outcome in Jackie's ordeal was the freedom she felt to move on with life, to grow, to change, to relate to others in spite of the fact that her relational cup was not full in her mind.

She was at liberty to become faithful to God even though life circumstantially had not been fair to her. That kind of freedom escapes most people who long for a relationship they never got.

The True Source of Relationship

The bottom line is that an unfulfilled person who isn't married will still be unfulfilled after the wedding. A dissatisfied individual without his dad's approval will still be dissatisfied with it! Changes in circumstances can put off our emptiness but it won't get rid of it

Often worldly relationships are similar to a child at the beach reaching down with his two hands cupped together to collect some water for his sand pile. When he begins to walk back from the water to his sand creation, his hands are brimming with water.

But by the time he returns to the mound of sand, most of the water has drained out. Human relationships work in a similar fashion. They appear to satisfy us at first but they are leaky at best. Relationship within this world is simply a taste of what only God can give.

If my wife is waiting for me to love her perfectly before she can be a ministering, caring, worthwhile woman and wife, she will have to wait for Heaven because I can't satisfy her needs all the time.

I try hard, but as imperfect partner I won't comply every time. She must understand that God is the only full and absolute source of ideal love, agape love. *"God is love,"* I John 4 tells us and no one is His equal.

Jackie possesses His wonderful love NOW, with or without me. My task, through my limited abilities, is to love her as much like Jesus as possible. But more importantly I need to point her to the Savior true head of our home.

He is the *perfect* bridegroom who gave Himself for all of us. She is then free to love me, inadequacies and all, for who I am, and yet not need to squeeze more out of me than I am capable of giving her.

I spoke recently with a woman in her forties who is just learning that she can do something that doesn't please her mother and still live! For years she has never thought it okay to disagree with mom for fear that mom wouldn't be pleased with her anymore.

Her mom has many wonderful qualities and has been a helpful confidante at times. However, due to significant abuse in the daughter's background, she was terrified at the thought of losing any relationship she did have with her mom.

You see, if you know Jesus as your personal Savior, you too have all the relationship you ultimately need in Him. Of course, you may want to get married - it is a wonderful and sacred experience.

And there is nothing wrong with deeply craving a parent's affections even after years of conflict, mistrust and disrespect.

You might be seeking more close friends and acquaintances who really do care about you. Being in a small group of caring, authentic and loving friends is *heavenly* in many ways.

We do need one another. God designed the church to be a place of ongoing compassion, accountability, relationship and encouragement. (NOTE: That spells C.A.R.E.)

However, when we begin to see God's ability to love us no know matter what we are like, we are freed to love others and enjoy relationship without milking each personal relationship for more than it can give.

Consider Arlene, a woman in her mid-twenties, who while growing up experienced very little love and appreciation from her father. Though she was never technically abused in a physical way, her dad would often tell her how poorly she was dressed, that she was overweight and that she probably wouldn't amount to much, especially considering the crowd she hung around.

Deep in the recesses of her heart, however, Arlene yearned just once for a loving response from her dad that told her she was lovable, that he noticed her as someone valuable and worthwhile.

As a teen she began to speculate, *"Is it me? Am I really not someone who my dad would ever compliment? Maybe I'm just not that lovable anyway."*

There are many scenarios Arlene could contemplate but one of those might be to get married. Arlene may begin to anticipate her husband becoming the restorer of the loving relationship she longed for from her dad. But then her husband must come through for her by always being loving and accepting, something which he could never possibly do.

And when he fails to be outwardly loving, she will gradually pull on the reins of their love ever tighter, demanding more and more that his human affections fill the huge void in her heart.

However, if Arlene can come to understand the depths of God's total and completely unconditional love for her, she will be liberated to passionately enjoy her spouse's love for what it is, even though it is tainted and incomplete at best.

Similarly, as each of us begins to understand God's unfailing love for us (it's called lovingkindness in the Bible) we can serve God now and see supernatural transformation in us, married or not, understood or not, cared for or not, with a partner or not.

What unfulfilled relationships are holding you back right now from exhilarating service to God? What relational somedays cause you to remain outside the doorway to meaningful change?

God told Judah through the prophet Jeremiah to, *"Break up your unplowed ground and do not sow among the thorns." (4:3)* Stop being dormant, begin to bear fruit again was the message. Finally, we read in chapter 31, *"I have loved you with an everlasting love; I have drawn you with lovingkindness."* Now that's true relationship!

Is God enough for you? Once more I suggest that you answer the question at the end of the chapter listing those relational demands that run your life right now. God is certainly not asking you to forget about those who mean much to you or to not feel the pain and sadness that they have brought you.

Rather, God is asking you to let go of the hold that they have on you, keeping you from freely serving Him and other. You can break their chains that stop you from joyful interaction other believers. People will no longer convince you that you are deficient and inadequate to accomplish meaningful tasks for God. Embrace the power of these incredible truths from the Bible:

"By this I will know that God is for me." (Psalm 56:9) The God of the universe is on your team! You do matter. You are loveable. You can leave a legacy that counts for eternity. You can change.

"He brought me out into a spacious place; he rescued me because he delighted in me." (Psalm 18:19) "The Lord your God is with you, he is mighty to save. He will take great delight in you, he will quiet you with his love, he will rejoice over you with singing." Zephaniah 3:17

No, we don't deserve our relationship with our Heavenly Father, but He loves us anyway. Jesus died and rose again so that we could enjoy intimacy, unconditional love and true relationship now and forever. Don't wait for someday to enjoy it.

As you attach yourself to God's unconditional love you will begin to experience a new liberty to enjoy your relationships for what they are and not for what you demand them to be. Start today.

Hopefully, as you've read these first three chapters you have gained some insight into what the *Someday Syndrome* looks like and just how you and your family may be impacted by it. Unfortunately, there is more to the human condition that just good intentions.

Our hearts are, *"Deceitful above all things and beyond cure. Who can understand it?"* (Jeremiah 17:9) Even as children of God our sinful natures can still be seduced to trust ourselves and not the living LORD of the universe.

Our self-centeredness is a powerful disease that continues to control our flight to the world of someday. In the next three chapters I want to examine a trio of cancers that will continue to attack us from the inside out, starting with FEAR.

Gary Sinclair

Things to Think About in Chapter 3

Who are your most treasured relationships right now? Why? What do you enjoy most about them?

What relationship is most lacking? What do you find yourself hoping, even demanding, will come from them **your way?**

What are you possibly putting off until *Someday* because they are not being all you want them to be?

Read again some of the key verses from this chapter and ponder what they mean to you about who you are in spite of relationship disappointments.

THE FUEL OF FEAR
CHAPTER 4

"I failed my way to success." Thomas Edison

There I was, my body clumsily swaying back and forth, supported only by my buckling knees and trembling feet, wobbling like a rag doll on a cable suspended between two trees some thirty-five feet above a swamp.

No, I wasn't part of an exotic African expedition or serving as a contestant on *Survivor.* I was taking part in a ropes course at a youth camp where I happened to be the speaker.

For several days I'd observed scores of upper-elementary, inner- city boys scamper their way across what was known as the *Burma Bridge,* a narrow set of cables high above rather murky waters. This challenge and others like it were helping them learn to defy their fears and enjoy a sense of accomplishment not normally found in their poverty-stricken neighborhoods of Detroit.

Having little fear of heights and wishing to impress my young listeners that week, I agreed to venture out onto the narrow metal cable which I was quickly termed the *Wire of Death.* To keep from falling, each participant was placed into a climber's harness connected by a rope and carabiner in the back to an overhead cable.

Although unseen by each wire walker, this connector moved along the upper cable as the participant inched forward, keeping him from plummeting into the swamp below.

On either side of the center cables were two additional ropes hanging loosely which could be used to assist with balance. After being fully secured and feeling quite confident, I gingerly, but nonetheless proudly, stepped onto the cable. To my surprise the first ten steps were quite uneventful as my youthful admirers shouted out praise and encouragement such as, "*Alright, Gary, go, man, go!*"

Within moments, however, I found myself starting to wobble on the sagging portion of the wire, the section with no central support, the part of the cable which simply swayed in the breeze. Instead of legs of steel, mine now felt like jelly.

As I bobbed up and down while leaning side to side, my head began to spin and my heart raced like an Indy-car as I wondered if I would ever see my family again!

After two or three stumbling steps both forward and backward, I found myself frozen half way across the bridge. I tightly clutched the side ropes, desperately warring against the forces of gravity to preserve my balance.

Confidence had now turned to fear, exhilaration to panic! I felt paralyzed and yet the cable continued to sway. Even my self-protecting near-fetal position only helped for a moment, as the forces of nature required me to constantly adjust and readjust my flailing body to stay upright. I must have looked like a Bobble-head doll on speed!

As I re-live that experience in my mind, I picture many Christians today, living in a similar position to mine on that cable: fearful, panicky, terrorized, dreading the thought of having to move forward. They hold instead to small bits of relationship, responsibility or security hoping that they will survive and somehow get through life.

Unfortunately, since the beginning of mankind, the cancer of fear has inwardly eaten away at the truth that would free them from the hospice of the *Someday Syndrome.*

Remember the story of Adam and Eve in the garden described in Genesis 3? God asked them why they had tried to camouflage themselves from Him and the first thing out of Adam's mouth was, *"I was afraid."*

Picture with me God's first two human creations, trembling behind God's greenery, hoping He wouldn't discover them. They were frozen by their fears, knowing that their sinfulness and inadequacies had been exposed. They stood, so to speak, on their *Eden Bridge,* hoping they wouldn't die.

It was fear of the giants that almost kept the children of Israel out of the Promised Land were it not for the courage of Joshua and Caleb. The remainder of the committee returned from spying out the land ready to turn in their warrior badges exclaiming, *"We can't attack those people, they are stronger than we are." (Numbers 13:31)*

Or consider Gideon whose fear demanded signs from God, a pair of fleeces, to convince him he could actually fight against the Midianites and win. (Judges 6) What profound words God uttered when he exhorted Gideon, *"Peace! Do not be afraid. You are not going to die." (6:23)* Fear is one of life's great paralyzers.

Each year thousands of deer are killed on America's highways because the startling bright lights of an automobile at dusk or twilight freeze the animal in its tracks only to face a likely death. And yet additional days or even years of life for that deer were only a movement away!

Fear keeps people from riding on airplanes, going to amusement parks, speaking in public, trying something new. But fear also inhibits service for God, healing of relationships and radical life change.

Dr. Erwin Lutzer, in his now classic book on emotions, agrees that fear *"can prevent you from enjoying life... can lock up deep inside the gifts that God has given you, never to be used."*

Could fear be one reason why in many churches in America today, a small percentage of the people are doing a major part of the work? *"I'd do that job but I probably wouldn't be very good at it,"* millions mutter to themselves.

Perhaps one of the most extreme forms of fear is the condition which overtakes thousands called *agoraphobia*. Although sometimes erroneously defined as a fear of crowds, it is more accurately described as a *fear of fear*.

Agoraphobics, who typically do not dare venture far from their homes, are terrified that they will be someplace in public like the mall, school, the work place and not know what to do or how to function at any given moment.

They panic at the thought of being out of control, dreading the possibility that they might be incompetent to handle some basic task like getting to their car, finding their way home or one of a hundred other seemingly normal human duties.

Because of their intense worry, they choose to become chained to a comfortable place, usually their house, selecting rather to endure the lonely isolation of their solitude over the risk of facing their own potential failures.

Fear again is the culprit.

Obviously, fear in and of itself isn't necessarily evil. For instance, I happen to possess what most people would say is an over-developed fear of snakes. Just deliver a garter snake to a room where I happen to be and I become nearly panic-stricken. In 2006, we moved to

Texas for eight years and sometimes wondered what we were thinking!

However, few would chastise me if I came face-to-face with a poisonous rattler and subsequently ran the fastest one-hundred-meter dash known to mankind in the other direction! My fear may have saved my life since that snake literally had the power to kill me!

Healthy fears of disease, terrorism, trucks hitting us in an intersection, hot stoves, and other potentially harmful objects or persons, help us to function more efficiently and safely in our everyday worlds.

We need to teach our children to have appropriate fears of many strangers, certain parts of the Internet and drugs confident that through our warnings we are protecting them to the best of our abilities from unnecessary evils.

But when our fears about life become debilitating and keep us from a meaningful life and service to God and others, we must allow Him to examine us at the core.

What is it that scares us so significantly that, like a deer, we can be stopped in our personal, emotional and spiritual tracks?

Shakespeare was evidently right when in Richard III he wrote: *"Truly, the souls of men are full of dread: Ye cannot reason almost with a man that looks not heavily and full of fear?"*

Fear comes in many shapes, sizes, quantities and emotional recesses deep within, but several will be common to most. The fear that started in the Garden of Eden still resides in most of us yet today.

Major Sources of Our Fears

The fear of failure.

No one likes to fail. But even worse, no one likes to come up short in front of someone else! Many of the greatest athletes and artists face major fears before a performance or game.

Haven't you at one time or another done something rather foolish and the first thing you did was to look around to see if someone else was looking? Recently, I got up from my office computer to go to another location in the building.

However, as I tried to weave my way around the corner of my desk, my foot caught on the leg which caused me to stumble over my wastebasket which sent me quickly to the floor! I can't remember the last time I've literally just fallen down!

I felt like such an idiot but I remember immediately looking towards the door to see if anyone had seen this classic moment of clumsiness and I quickly prayed that no one had heard the thud!

Or chances are that you and I have lied a time or two to a parent, friend, or colleague to make our blunder appear less foolish or to completely cover it up. Even our educational system with its emphasis on tests, quizzes, grade-point averages and special awards makes failure, experimentation and creative thinking substandard to a computer-like memory.

Having lived in the Detroit area for a significant part of my life, I couldn't help but be impacted by the automobile industry. Interestingly, when taking tours of the auto plants we were usually told about the millions of dollars that were spent each year on trial and error, research and planned failure.

We now know that Edison, Ford, Lincoln, Einstein and scores of other great minds were failures more times than they were successes. And yet we as humans dodge any form of failure like a fatal disease. Why?

Much of the answer lies in our past, painful experiences, times when we failed miserably and people noticed. Most of us can remember events and situations where failure hurt us to the very depths of our personhood. Somehow, we believed that our mistakes made us less valuable or not worth being loved or accepted.

A teacher called us stupid, a parent implied we weren't very skillful, a friend laughed at our lack of knowledge about something everyone supposedly knows.

When Jane came to see me, she was in her mid-twenties. As our counseling progressed, I asked her if there was ever an event or series of circumstances in her life that she painfully remembered from childhood and would likely never forget.

Without even pausing, she began to recount a story from her elementary school days. It seems that one quarter of the school year during the third grade she received a 'D' on her report card, an outcome she knew full well would not please her parents. She decided that she would change the 'D' to a 'B,' not comprehending in her eight-year-old mind that a parent would immediately notice the forgery.

And of course, they did notice, harshly reprimanding Jane and returning her quarterly evaluation to the teacher as was required of each student. Upon Jane's arrival back to class, however, the teacher vented her disappointment with Jane and quickly ushered her off to the principal's office.

As luck (or misfortune) would have it, the principal was not available at the moment and Jane was told to sit and wait. The minutes turned into an hour or more and Jane needed to use the bathroom, but her trepidation glued her to her seat. Instead she wet her pants right there in the office.

The principal finally arrived and severely chided Jane, not only for her dishonesty, but also for the soaking of her underwear and the chair. As punishment Jane was told to march herself across the hall to one of the upper-elementary classrooms and stand at attention next to the blower on the heating unit until her pants were dry.

Before the leering eyes of an entire classroom Jane felt her dignity and worth evaporate into thin air, overwhelmed by her shame and embarrassment.

Jane was able during our talks to look back and visualize her determined resolve from that point on to never, ever fail again, particularly when in plain view of anyone else.

There were subsequently few risks in Jane's life - no cheerleader tryouts, no attempts to learn new skills or sports, no pursuit of fresh relationships unless initiated by others. Jane was committed to never feel deep, soul-touching, pain like that again!

And most of us respond to past hurts in the very same way. We will hide from failure no matter the cost. Like Adam and Eve in Genesis 3 we too cower behind seemingly good plans, projects or skills.

The first humans hid behind the very bushes which God made! Our shrubbery today may be church work, evangelistic ministry, helping others in need, always being nice, performing music, volunteer service or a thousand other things.

Sadly, the majority of our actions become mere performances, hideaways that we demand keep us from the searing torment of our past inadequacies. Often to those who have failed too often and been hurt too deeply, even *somedays* are out of the question. Instead they become *no ways.* That happened to Jane during much of her life. *"No way will I ever fail again and be humiliated by it,"* was her subconscious mantra.

Although she lived an active life, Jane spent almost twenty years of her existence missing the joy of growing, learning and experiencing new things.

Fear of Rejection

Although rejection is a form of failure it deserves special attention at this point. We tend to think of failure in terms of skills and behaviors while rejection relates more to our inside, our personage or personhood.

I can fail at an entrance test for graduate school and still potentially feel okay as a father. But if my son tells me he doesn't love me anymore, I now feel rejected as a person.

A young man can be cut by the basketball team and still sense his worth is intact the next week (although this can still be difficult for an adolescent). But if he believes he can never develop a close friendship, he will likely experience intense rejection as a human being.

A wife may not be the great cook she's always desired to be, but when her husband has an affair with another woman, waves of personal rejection flood her soul. Rejection is what a teenager feels when her parents' divorce and she wonders if it was her fault.

It is what parents endure when a child leaves home and refuses to come back. It is what a husband experiences when his wife will not accept his role in leadership and undermines his every effort to help train up his children in the way they should go.

Somehow rejection penetrates to the very joints and marrow of our being leading us to believe that nothing we could ever do in our present condition would be enough to make us okay.

Proverbs tells us a multitude of times that our words have great power. *"The tongue has the power of life and death, and those who love it will eat its fruit."* (18:21) *"The words of a gossip are like choice morsels; they go down to a man's inmost parts."* (18:8)

Words, and the images from our past they conjure up, form the core of our fear of being discarded. To most of us, rejection makes us feel like some part of ourselves deep within us has died.

As a result, we live much of our life running or hiding from potential banishment as we would flee a cancer that slowly eats away at our flesh. We feel powerless to move into the lives of others and make a difference.

Consequently, we are unwilling to risk trying anything new. We keep emotions controlled, accomplishments high, and mistakes minimized so we will never again taste the anguish of being put aside or shunned by someone in our world.

I will never forget Phil, a father in his mid-forties, who sat in the circle with eight of us each week as a part of a seminary group counseling class. One week, Phil began to tell us how he longed to become close to his son, to wrestle on the floor, pat him on the back, tussle his hair, give him a bear hug or even a kiss.

But through tears of despair, Phil related how he never had the courage to approach his son and risk a negative response. Would his boy walk away, make a smart remark, think dad was stupid, and be embarrassed? Would he say the right things, not overdo it, and be as understanding as he should?

I also think of Carl, a ninth-grade student whose grades were simply horrid. His parents and the school had tried every motivational technique known to mankind to get Carl's schoolwork to improve. Nothing worked. After Carl and I had talked for a while, I inquired about why he didn't do his homework and I'll never forget his response. *"Mr. Sinclair, I do my homework most of the time. I just don't turn it in."*

"Why?" I responded, pressing him further.

"Because usually when my work comes back it's full of red marks and I just hate seeing that." You see Carl couldn't face the scarlet reminders of how much he didn't know! Instead he chose to enjoy less painful living now and to endure the wrath of his parents later.

Like Carl, most of us would rather smolder in the ashes of mediocrity and meaningless existence than to face the burning flames of personal rejection. Instead we settle for *someday*.

Handling Our Fears

What do we do if fear really does have us stymied and we are held in the clutches of the *Someday Syndrome?* Although an overly simplistic answer isn't appropriate, follow me back to my sojourn on the *Burma Bridge.*

For what seemed like minutes (though it may have only been seconds) I battled ferociously to retain my equilibrium. And I was NOT about to conclude my adventure hanging upside down under the attentive eyes of my campers!

Soon, however, I began to hear the voice of one of the leaders behind me yelling loudly. He slowly spoke these words that I'll never forget: *"Push the ropes out away from your body and keep moving, push the ropes out and keep moving!"*

My immediate reaction was, *"Are you nuts?"*

What he was suggesting was the exact opposite of what everything within me screamed to do! My fearful instincts instead shouted, *"Pull the ropes in, Gary, and stop where you are, pull the ropes in and be safe!"*

All I wanted at that moment was for someone to come and rescue me from this terror.

Nevertheless, my wise leader knew that NOW was the time for me to succeed. If I was to make progress, I was going to have to embrace some fundamental changes both in my thinking and my behavior. And so, through my desperation, I carefully began to push the cables clutched in my palms outward and to once again inch my feet along the lower one.

Remarkably, I began to achieve greater, though still shaky, balance. I continued to wobble but soon stood a bit taller. My eyes looked ahead instead of downward and I saw so much more. I was able to look beyond my own predicament.

I again heard the encouragement of the boys and their counselors yelling, *"C'mon, Gary, you can do it!"* My energy was jump-started and I surged ahead, stumbling yes, but more confidently making my way to the other side.

As I triumphantly stood on what became my victor's platform, four stories above the swamp, I experienced what I can only term as *exhilarating terror*. Terror, yes, due to my close encounter with death; exhilarating because I had survived something bigger than myself, defeating a foe I had never encountered before.

As it was, I could not have fallen to my death. The harness and the unseen rope behind me prevented that. But I had moved from a belief that I must rescue myself from the fear to the thought that I could actually overcome my fear and accomplish a goal beyond my belief. After my success, the exhilaration won out and I actually wanted to try it again!

The Power of the Rope

I have become convinced that moving from someday to today resembles my cable-crossing adventure on the *Burma Bridge*. Although I will talk later in more detail about how we can radically change, I want to address how to begin to escape from the power of our fear.

Overcoming our fears as Christians and living out God's biblical plan for our lives mandates that we encounter at times what I earlier referred to as *exhilarating terror*. We will have to step out in obedience knowing that alone we cannot accomplish the task, all the while hanging precariously over the swamp of rejection and failure. In fact, at times we actually do splash into the swamp of rejection and failure but God pulls us out.

There is an unseen rope that sustains and supports and protects us. The rope has two strands: God's unconditional love for us and the worth, value or impact that he freely gives every one of His children. These two strands intertwine and are fastened to each believer by God through the power of His Holy Spirit the moment we become one of His children through faith in Christ.

Ephesians 1:13, 14 reminds us that, *"Having also believed, you were sealed in Him with the Holy Spirit of promise, who is given as a pledge of our inheritance, with a view to the redemption of God's own possession, to the praise of His glory."* God has promised He would never let us go!

As I stood in the center of that span above an ugly quagmire, I sensed that I was not going to die. As a result, I took a step or two, pushing the ropes out as I went. As I inched forward, I knew death was not imminent and consequently I kept moving with more confidence.

We also must listen to God as He speaks to us regarding our safety and position in His care. Here are a few samples:

Psalm 56:3,4, "When I am afraid, I will trust in You. In God, whose word I praise, In God I trust; I will not be afraid. What can mortal man do to me?"

Psalm 37:23, "If the Lord delights in a man's way, he makes his steps firm; though he stumble, he will not fall, for the LORD upholds him with his hand."

Psalm 31:21, "Praise be to the LORD, for he showed his wonderful love to me when I was in a besieged city."

If we never risk or lean to the side, we won't test the power of the rope. Unfortunately, many Christians live life just that way, safe and never needing to wonder if God will actually hold them up. They are more like the jet pilot who won't cross the imaginary point of no return on the runway in case something goes wrong.

How do YOU play it safe these days? Are you convicted that you need to be a helper in the children's ministry but still unwilling to risk making a mistake in front of others? Perhaps you're burdened that you should approach a neighbor with your coming to Christ story but you're afraid that they won't want your friendship anymore?

Have you been challenged to quit taking responsibility for everyone else's actions and responses at work and yet unwilling to enjoy an extra day off for fear of a reprimand? Has there been a quiet urging to serve in some other ministry and yet you're fearful of what others will say?

II Timothy I:7 says, *"For God has not given us a spirit of timidity (fear), but of power and love and discipline."* Romans 8:15 teaches us to abhor anything that binds us from service, *"For you have not received a spirit of slavery leading to fear again, but you have received a spirit of adoption as sons by which we cry out, 'Abba! Father.'"*

The key to victory over fear is not to live without it but to keep moving forward in spite of it!

Moving Step by Step

Have you ever noticed how often the word *walk* is used in the Scriptures? The New Testament alone refers to numerous walks that the believer is required to undertake. Some translations use the word *live* but the meaning is the same.

There is the *walk of faith* (Hebrews 10:38), *the walk in love* (2 John 6), *the walk in the light* (I John 1:7), *the walk in truth* (2 John 4), *the walk in the Spirit* (Galatians 5:16).

And even though Paul refers at one point to *running the race* (I Corinthians 9:24) he, along with the writer of Hebrews (12: 1,2), implies that the Christian race is more like a marathon than a sprint.

In other words, following Christ is not a short-term commitment. There is ample room for mistakes, patience, slowing down and speeding up. Living for Christ is dramatically closer to a long walk than a short run. And overcoming our fears will fundamentally require a step-by-step journey if we are to ever going to enjoy progress in the Christian life.

In an earlier chapter I alluded to my love for the mountains and Jackie's inspirational climb to a summit before her cancer. Another part of that story was born many years ago now.

Lessons from the mountains

Over fifteen summers ago my then thirteen-year-old son Tim and I climbed *Long's Peak*, the highest mountain in *Rocky Mountain National Park*. Our ascent was the culmination of a 30-year dream to return to *Long's* and conquer it. *Long's* became the first of nine fourteeners I've summited with either one or both of my kids, a friend or my wife.

It was a wonderful experience, even though my then forty-one-year- old body had not done anything so demanding in at least twenty years! Nonetheless, this was a very long hike, eight miles each way and a thirteen-hour trip total. For the first six miles we hiked, up and up and up, step by step. We moved along pretty well.

But soon we reached the actual mountain and our pace slowed significantly. We climbed over boulders and across ledges. Later we were forcing ourselves up the side of the mountain fighting against the pull of gravity, stopping every twenty feet or so to gasp for more oxygen. Even Tim was tired!

We kept urging each other on between gulps of fluids, *"Let's just go another few feet. We can't quit now."* And we didn't. The view from the summit was spectacular and suddenly the pain seemed not so intense. Step by step we had reached our goal, even though all of our steps were not equal. Together we learned in a most challenging way that the Christian life is a long walk that is worth it!

On another hike that included both Tim and Amy, we all inched our way up a different 14er, this time encountering 30-50 mile an hour wind gusts most of the way up and down. What was to be a much easier climb than *Longs* at times felt like *K2*! You can read more about the lessons high altitude climbing can teach us in my book *Never Quit Climbing*.

Contemplate this unusual passage in Deuteronomy 7:22, *"And the Lord your God will clear away these nations before you little by little; you will not be able to put an end to them quickly, lest the wild beasts grow too numerous for you."*

Do the Scriptures actually say God was going to drive out the enemy nations a little bit at a time? Why doesn't God simply say the word and destroy them all in an instant?

God chose to go slowly for the sake of the people. He could handle the instant devastation but God knew the people certainly could not. With so many dead in such a short time, the predators would have overtaken the countryside and those He loved would have been in danger.

In a similar manner, God chooses to allow us to change and progress little by little. He promised us the power and strength to take the next step or two, whatever He and we can handle. We do not have to start with the mountain. We can do a foothill first.

If you are afraid of ministry but sense God challenging you to get involved, don't first think about going overseas. Start with something small within your church or community such as helping out, offering volunteer time, working alongside a capable veteran and learning the basics of ministry from them.

If you're nervous about confronting a major issue in your own life, try starting with a smaller one such as talk to your pastor, a counselor, a friend, etc. and begin to expose what you fear most. Be ready to lean a little while you experience the firm pull of God's rope in the process. You may experience some initial terror.

But don't stop there. *Never stop climbing.* Eventually go all the way. Let God walk with you through the dark valleys and up steep places keeping you going when everything inside begs you to quit.

Someone has wisely said, *"He who fears God need fear nothing else, and he who fears not God needs to fear everything else."* (*Anonymous*)

What you will find as you begin to walk in faith is that God's rope will hold and the balance between exhilaration and terror will begin to shift. At first your excursions into new behaviors will likely bring great anxiety and only brief exhilaration.

However, as you repeat your actions and let God begin to change your thinking, discovering that you really will not die in spite of the risks, you will become less panicky and more invigorated. You will feel much like the snow skier who never thought he could ski the big hill but now can't wait to tackle it again and again.

People who experience emotional freedom from their fears become more alive, invigorated and passionate again. Their lifestyle takes on a richness and depth that infects others and draws them into relationship. Life begins to move again, not wildly or foolishly, but with purpose and direction. God becomes so much more real.

Christ seems to be living in them again, not just a distant person or being. They are drawn to Him even in their most unattractive moments.

"Do not be fainthearted or afraid; do not be terrified or give way to panic before them. For the Lord your God is the one who goes with you to fight for you against your enemies to give you victory." *(Deuteronomy 20:3)*

God's Holy Spirit is can also be freed to minister in you. Bible study becomes more significant and we experience a regular hunger for more of God's Word. We will identify with the Davids, Daniels, Pauls, and Peters who in the midst of weakness and failure were used of God to carry out His purposes and add to His kingdom.

When Jesus' disciples were being pounded and battered by the waves of the sea, Jesus walked towards them along the surface of the water.

Matthew 14:26ff tells us that, *"When the disciples saw Him walking on the sea, they were frightened, saying, 'It is a ghost!' And they cried out for fear."* Later Peter took his famous stroll out onto the water with Jesus, and, *"Seeing the wind, he became afraid and began to sink.*" But Jesus reaches out with his strong arm and lifts him to safety.

We can face our own fears, our private wave-laden sea of problems and potential pain, and have this same Savior hold on to us with his outstretched arms! While Paul ministered in Corinth many of his Jewish detractors, "*resisted and blasphemed,*" causing Paul to lament, *"From now on I shall go to the Gentiles."* (Acts 18:6)

However, God soon spoke to Paul in a vision reminding him of his freedom to move on, even in the middle of his fear and discouragement, *"Do not be afraid; keep on speaking, do not be silent; for I am with you, and no one is going to attack and harm you, because I have many people in this city." (Acts 18: 9, 10)*

Are you in the middle of your *Burma Bridge* frozen by your fears and unable to move? Take some time to honestly identify those fears that are keeping you from the joy of your salvation and meaningful change. Begin to take small steps pushing out on the ropes and walking forward. God's rope of love is enough! Fear has no right to defeat you or me.

Like Adam and Eve, we can come out from behind the bushes of false security and face God Himself, exposed for all we are, and still fall into His loving arms which both protect us and prod us onward.

This monumental truth is so beautifully penned in the hymn, "*Oh, For a Thousand Tongues to Sing." Jesus! The name that charms our fears, That bids our sorrows cease, 'Tis music in the sinner's ears, 'Tis life and health and peace.*

Ironically, some people's somedays are not fueled as much by fear as they are by FANTASY, which we'll look at next.

Things to Think About in Chapter 4

Identify and list the fears you face from day to day. Try to divide them into two categories – *"Fears Which I Overcome Easily," "Fears Which Tend to Paralyze Me."*

Read through Psalm 56 and list those things God promises us to help us face our fears. Jot down specific ideas that encourage you.

Choose one of your paralyzing fears and identify a first step which you could take with God's help to face that fear and begin to conquer it.

THE FUEL OF FANTASY
CHAPTER 5

"I'm half living my life between reality and fantasy at all times."
Lady Gaga

It was my junior year of high school and our basketball team was rated #1 in the state for the entire season. What a fun time to be a fan and a student at East Detroit High School! During pep rallies the rafters would vibrate as the deafening cheers for our team engulfed the players running out onto the court.

My friends and I would marvel at their acrobatic dunks and precision ball-handling drills, imagining that we were out there on the court along with them.

This top-notch squad easily made their way through the initial tournaments and advanced to the state playoffs in East Lansing. *"We've been number one all year so we'll finish number one,"* we bragged to whoever would listen.

I was disappointed that I couldn't attend the semifinal game against Ferndale High School due to my own church league game. So, after our game was over, I hurried home to watch it on tape delay, the only option before ESPN and *OnDemand*.

Of course, I knew we had won but I couldn't wait to know by how much. But before I could watch, someone called and said they had heard that we lost. Ferndale 65, East Detroit 64.

I couldn't believe it! What had happened? How could the number one team in the state lose? I remember heading downstairs to my basement to watch the game hoping the information I got in that phone call was untrue.

As I started to watch the replay, I was optimistic. In fact, my team was winning! They were playing as though they were on a mission, not as a group who were about to suffer defeat. I found my hopes rising, confident that the report I had heard was just a mistake. I knew it. We were on our way to the state final game.

With a bowl of hot buttered popcorn in my lap and a Coke in hand I sat back and waited for my guys to wrap this one up and move on to the finals. At one point in the second half we were ahead by as much as ten points, confirming my conviction that East Detroit High had won.

However, with just minutes to go my confidence returned to despair as I watched Ferndale claw their way back into the game, steal several errant passes and make a final shot just before the buzzer to win. Yes, we had lost by one point.

Even though I knew better, I had convinced myself that the outcome would be different. In my mind it couldn't have ended the way I'd heard it on the radio. I refused to believe the truth even as I watched the taped rerun.

Decades later, I sat with millions around the world watching the Challenger explosion shown on the various news outlets over and over and over.

I remember thinking to myself, "*Just play the video one time, please, where the shuttle doesn't blow up!*" How silly, but oh how much we wanted things to be different. More recent tragedies in New York, Washington and London brought similar, but no less unrealistic, hopes to many.

For sufferers of the *Someday Syndrome*, fantasy can be another factor that prevents them from movement forward, commitment or meaningful change. They believe with all their hearts that somehow, some way, a part of their world is going to be dramatically altered and only then can they move to a better, healthier way of living.

C.S. Lewis cleverly illustrates this devilish human tendency in his delightful, yet poignant book, *The Screwtape Letters*. While trying to train his neophyte demon nephew Screwtape regarding the intricacies of temptation, Uncle Wormwood gives advice on how to undermine Christian commitment and effectiveness.

"Our business is to get them away from the eternal and from the present . . . It is far better to make them live in the Future. Biological necessity makes all their passions point in that direction already, so that thought about the Future inflames hope and fear. Also, it is unknown to them, so that in making them think about it we make them think of unrealities."

Spouses of alcoholics typically live in their own Disney World lifestyle, assured that one day soon the drinker will give up his or her booze and finally be the person they knew they could be. As a result, a wife typically endures one more night of irresponsibility, one more carrying-him-to-bed scenario, one more excuse given to a boss about why he didn't arrive at work that day.

And like alcohol, fantasy dulls the mind to the realities of life, seducing the Christian into believing everything is going to one day work out fine.

And yet King David, following perhaps the most grievous of his sins, adultery with Bathsheba, reminds us that God desires most our HONESTY, not our pretensions that all is well: *"Surely you desire truth in the inner parts; you teach me wisdom in the inmost place."* (Psalm 51:6)

And in another similar song David writes, *"Lord, who may dwell in your sanctuary? Who may live on your holy hill? He whose walk is blameless and who does what is righteous, who speaks the truth from his heart..."* (Psalm 15:1, 2)

Fantasy in Action

Angela was an attractive, well-dressed, and successful business woman, a wife of three kids, who in recent months had come to know Christ as her Savior and was growing in her faith. She was also married at one time to an alcoholic and sex addict named Dan.

For years Angela, though admittedly not a perfect wife, longed for Dan to spend time with her and the children, but Dan's work and other chosen responsibilities kept him away much of the time. Glowing promises from Dan to the family were constantly broken and when confronted, Dan flew into a rage.

Dan also regularly demanded sex from his wife, often in forms that Angela found distasteful, prompted by his wanderings into pornography. Nevertheless, she gave in most of the time, only to feel humiliated and guilt-ridden over her reluctance to say "*no.*"

As we talked over a several month period, it became clear that Angela's world was governed by illusion, not reality. She had pictured herself since childhood living in a country-style home with several wonderful children and a loving husband at her side, supported by a handsome income, all eating home-cooked meals together, attending church every Sunday while living happily ever after.

In Angela's mind, Dan's imperfections were only temporary, a nightmare at times, but she would awaken soon and all would be wonderful. Her pain and suffering were but a small price to pay for the bliss that was sure to follow.

Unfortunately, Dan never changed. In fact, Dan was, as heavy drinkers often are, unaware that he needed to change at all. He didn't believe he was an alcoholic in the first place and wanted Angela to give him some time to prove himself. When offered the opportunity to receive specialized help, he stubbornly refused.

Angela is perhaps one of the saddest types of *Someday Syndrome* fantasizers, because like many others capsized by the waves of mistreatment, she tolerates ongoing abusive and self- destructive behaviors, desperately hoping and believing that her abuser will change.

Of course, some might ask, *"But doesn't God have the power to change someone like Dan? Shouldn't Angela have just prayed more and trusted God for the result?"* I would certainly be one of the first to agree that God does have the power to change Dan. Angela's godly spirit and behavior might have won him over to Christ.

However, in this case, Angela's fantasizing reinforced Dan's irresponsibility and misuse of his relationship with her. Tolerating more pain and abuse only encouraged him to pile more of the same on Angela and the children.

It was only when Angela didn't demand that Dan change first anymore that she was able to break the cycle of her fantasy-driven and self-demeaning lifestyle. Dan also was forced to squarely face his own culpability and choose whether he was going to appropriately love and care for Angela or not.

The pain-killing power of fantasy

In novels, movies and amusement parks fantasy can be a wonderful, exciting and just plain fun form of entertainment, provided it doesn't promote the occult or other Satanic or spirit-world ideas. Taking our kids to Disney World a number of years ago now and watching the glows on their faces as they met Donald Duck and Minnie Mouse was a wonderful experience for Jackie and me.

Years later, the two of us visited Universal Studios and rode through the ET exhibit, flying through the countryside on ET's bicycle. For five minutes or so I forgot all the troubles of the world, the pressures of my job and the people with whom I struggled. How I wished for a while that the ride would never end.

More recently millions have enjoyed the *Lord of the Rings* trilogy in movie form. Wholesome fantasy can provide wonderful hours of fun, excitement and wonder when offered in the right setting and enjoyed in moderation.

Nevertheless, some fantasy has a much more serious and often devastating effect on people. It anesthetizes them from reality. It helps to dull the pain of what is.

Today an ever-increasing percentage of men, even Christian men (and some women) and full-time Christian workers in many cases, are obsessed with pornography. The easy availability on the Internet of pornographic and sensual pictures today have without question lured more victims into this tangled web. Many have sacrificed their jobs, reputations and ministries to enjoy the fantasy of a virtual and sometimes real sexual experience for a few moments, hours, days or months.

But my counseling and pastoral experience shows that most men who dabble or become entrapped by pornography and its related attractions, are not enjoying intimacy in their marriage or other social relationships.

Pornography, a sexual fantasy, or other explicit materials became their substitute for genuine closeness which had severely threatened them for one reason or another. The air-brushed woman in the magazine or the scantily clad beauty on the computer screen never said "no" nor did she ever reject him for his lousy personality, fat stomach or unattractive facial features.

Those few moments with this pretend woman or women help dull the pain that his hollowness had produced within him earlier that day or week.

For a woman, relational fantasies usually come in forms other than pornography since women are typically less visually- oriented. (Note: As I implied above, recent studies are showing more and more women can also be addicted to pornography, but their numbers are still fewer).

Females are more likely to envision their husband bringing them flowers, going on a surprise romantic weekend or, like Angela, one day having a nice family and home. They may dream of the time when their spouse finally lands that promotion and then the family will have time together.

Tragically, some women envision getting a man who affectionately cares for them, compliments them and puts them first, only to meet someone else at work, church or nearby who appears to be just that man and ends up ruined by a family-destroying affair.

Like any painkiller, fantasy can make the hurt from an unfulfilling relationship disappear for a while. But the anguish eventually returns, prompting the cycle of anesthetizing to begin again. Fantasizers are much like a spinning top, whizzing and bobbing, but, in reality, going nowhere.

The Focus of our Fantasies

Although there are literally thousands of examples, most of our fantasies can be grouped into several common arenas. *Someday Syndrome* people tend to believe that before they can move on with life one or more of the following must occur.

Someone else must change.

Like the wife of the alcoholic many Christians are waiting for another person in their world to finally become the person they had hoped. *"When the pastor starts preaching the Word . . . ," "When my father sees me for who I really am . . . ," "When my wife starts complimenting me instead of griping all the time . . . ,"* are typical statements from people paralyzed by un-fulfilled fantasies.

Consider your own dreams about others becoming new people. Who are you waiting for to get it together? A church leader, your spouse, your child's school teacher, your boss, a neighbor, the kids, government officials, the pastor, a friend, another team member, a coworker?

Have you ever thought to yourself something like, *"I just hate this job! My supervisor is arrogant, pig-headed and self-centered. No one likes him so why should I? I'll put in my time but I might as well resign myself to the fact that I'm stuck with him until he leaves or I die."*

Do you hear the tires of your life screeching to a halt as you think that way? If so, then you've handed over power to enjoy your life to your boss on a silver platter and said, *"Here, take my ability to be happy and do with it as you please. If you don't change, I'll be miserable, but if you do maybe there is hope for me."*

Actor Woody Allen says it well, *"In real life people disappoint you. They are cruel, and life is cruel. I think there is no win in life. Reality is a very painful, tough thing that you have to learn and cope with in some way. What we do is escape into fantasy, and it does give us moments of relief."*

Christians are immobilized all the time from serving in their churches because, *"The pastor isn't quite my style,"* or, *"The board doesn't listen to me enough,"* or, *"They never choose me to teach."*

Obviously it can be appropriate to graciously, lovingly and even firmly seek changes in pastors, leadership, working conditions and other less than desirable situations. However, those committed to a someday lifestyle don't merely seek change, they REQUIRE it.

Their message is loud and clear . . . *"If so and so becomes different, I'll change."* Unfortunately, these changes in others are largely out of our control, so as *Someday Syndromers* we merely become puppets manipulated by the choices, both good and bad, of others.

And yet since the days of Adam, man has been given a choice to make his or her own decisions in spite of what others do or don't do.

Adam for instance was responsible to name the animals. Joshua urged the children of Israel to *"choose for yourselves today whom you will serve."* (Joshua V24:15) Even our salvation is predicated on our freedom to choose to trust in Christ just as Paul told the Romans, *"For whoever will call upon the name of the Lord will be saved."* (10:13)

Or as John wrote, *"But as many as received Him to them He gave the right to become children of God, even to those who believe in His name."* (1:12) We must grab hold of our freedom to act boldly and right, in spite of others' irresponsibility or sinful states, through the power of God and because of His wonderful love for us.

No other person's lack of action or change need keep us from moving forward.

Some circumstance must change.

How many times have you said to yourself or a close friend or acquaintance:

"What I need is: A new church, a more attractive body, a different job, nicer neighbors, more money, more talent, a bigger house, additional time, more friends, a better education, deeper Bible knowledge" or whatever." "If only my surroundings were different," we lament. *"If only I weren't the way I am, then I could truly change my situation and life wouldn't be as horrible as it is right now."*

Married couples often dream that a change in something will solve all their problems. Wives wish their husbands dressed better, had more mechanical abilities, studied the Bible more, remembered anniversaries, quit drinking and didn't watch sports so much.

Husbands likewise dream about wives who keep the house neater, take better care of themselves, get sexier, like to participate in sports, stay home more and cook gourmet meals every night.

Gary Sinclair

As we discussed earlier, singles often demand that marriage be their ticket to relational happiness and married couples think life will be fruitless without children. Students wish for higher educational degrees and senior citizens long for more energy or better health.

And yet, if we are ever to escape the paralysis of living in *Tomorrowland*, we must come to accept the following: *There is no circumstance or possession in this world that will ever totally satisfy us.* Even if the changes we desire do occur, they can never by themselves make us truly happy, contented or fulfilled.

Watch a child with a new toy. The new plaything seems so captivating for an hour, a day, a week, maybe even a month. But many times, the luster of its attraction begins to diminish within minutes of its being received.

That new car that we cherished becomes tarnished and routine before we know it. The diploma on our wall represents an important and hard-earned achievement and deserves our appropriate pride for our hard work. But to obtain it doesn't fill the empty crevasses in our hearts.

It's taken me a long time and I'm far from perfect, but anything I thought would ultimately make me happy now results in my eventually responding, *"This ain't it!"*

Not my wife, not my kids, not this book, not my job, not anything. Only God is capable of providing total soul-contentment and we only experience that on a limited scale anyway.

Could this be what David spoke of when he wrote: *"O taste and see that the LORD is good; How blessed is the man who takes refuge in Him." (Psalm 34:8)*

In spite of those limited tastes of God in His fulness, Psalm 107: 8, 9 says: *"Let them give thanks to the Lord for His unfailing love and his wonderful deeds for men, for he satisfies the thirsty and fills the hungry with good things."* We can accumulate all we want and more, our circumstances can turn wonderful for a time and yet it will always fall short.

90

Some behavior or ability must be altered.

We all want to be something or someone we're not. It's part of the human condition. If we're pretty we want to be prettier, if we're athletic we still want to be faster or stronger, if we're intelligent we seek more knowledge anyway.

In our household I started a tradition of writing songs for our children on their birthdays up through age twelve. It began when I wrote something for them after they were born, expressing the deep emotions that only a parent can experience after they see that new life come into the world.

But Tim, our oldest, liked to sit on the piano bench next to me most evenings and I would make up a song for him just for fun.

After a while, however, I ran out of ideas so I decided to start writing things down for them each year instead. Sometimes the lyrics were silly, while other times the messages became fairly profound. Nonetheless, every birthday we always had lots of fun enjoying these special compositions.

As Tim was approaching his seventh birthday, however, I sensed in him the typical little boy desires to be older, taller, and quicker, especially as sports became more important to him. He was always trying to see how high he could jump, constantly leaving his fingerprints visible above every doorway.

I also remembered the days in my own childhood when I, too, couldn't wait to be a certain height or the right age to drive on my own.

As I pondered what those feelings might be like for Tim, I wrote him a song which we all still laugh about called, *"I've Got The Just Turned Seven, Going on Eleven, But I Wish I Were Sixteen Blues."*

I think the words get at some of the sadness that we all face when we just don't quite measure up to our personal expectations. Here are the lyrics:

I'VE GOT THE JUST TURNED SEVEN, GOIN' ON ELEVEN, BUT I WISH I WERE SIXTEEN BLUES.

Verse 1
Bein' so little, I get stuck in the middle,
If I were a little older it would help.
Then I could stuff a basketball, but for that you must be tall,
I just can't keep my feelings to myself.

Chorus

You see I can't be older than I am right now,
But a few more years I wouldn't refuse,
I've got the just-turned-seven-goin' on-eleven-but-I-wish-I-were sixteen blues.

Verse 2

Havin' a new birthday I know I should be thrilled,
And I have to admit it's pretty great,
But I've got this new feeling that I've never had before,
It seems that being small just doesn't rate.

Verse 3

Now I'm one year older and a little bit bolder,
But I wouldn't mind growin' an inch or two,
Then I could climb a higher tree,
A whole lot farther I could see,
And perhaps I'd even be as tall as you!

Chorus

Verse 4

So, don't get me wrong,
I really like being seven,
But in my heart, I want much more,
To one day stay up late and even go on a date,
And some day drive myself and my sister to the store.

Repeat Chorus

©Gary Sinclair, 1985

We all have our own version of the not-good-enough blues, don't' we? *"I'd be a better spouse if I could just communicate better,"* we say to ourselves, frustrated during another marital spat. *"If I just knew more about the Bible,"* we bemoan, *"then I could be a bigger help to the church." "If I could get my weight under control then my husband would be more attracted to me."*

God must sometimes wonder, *"Since when did I require a seminary degree for ministry to occur, since when did it take eloquence to make a rich and harmonious marriage, since when is the ability to diet a prerequisite for family closeness?"*

God isn't dependent on our personal changes or behavioral resources to do His work. Communication skills, weight loss, and greater knowledge of the scriptures are all wise pursuits which assist us in our abilities to function, grow, or minister, but no behavioral change or ability is required to serve the God! *"Ah, Sovereign Lord, You have made the heavens and the earth by your great power and outstretched arm! Nothing is too hard for you." (Jeremiah 32:17)*

God can use us as we are, even if we're in the process of still working on ourselves. *We don't have to be all that we will be someday to be all that God desires us to do and be NOW!*

Gary's Story

I have never been much of a mechanically- minded person and for years that haunted me, starting during my history as a young child. My favorite playmate and buddy was Terry, my cousin of the same age, who I believe was given the spiritual gift of *mechanicalness*. (Okay, there probably isn't one of those gifts but it sure was a talent.)

But, unintentionally, his skills also reinforced my bad feelings about my ineptitude for nuts and bolts and things related.

When we were about ten or so, I recall Terry coming over to the house one day to do something fun together. Our toaster at the time was broken and my mom happened to mention our problem during lunch. Terry fixed it! On the other hand, I was lucky if I could just make toast!

My parents bought me one of those *Erector Sets* (which by the way recently sold on eBay in perfect condition) hoping I would somehow absorb a speck or two of mechanical acumen from it.

I recall a Sunday afternoon sitting with Terry in a room somewhere. While I had pieced together a couple of metal rods connected by several nuts and bolts, I discovered that Terry during the same time period had assembled the *Golden Gate Bridge* (or at least something comparable)!

When on one occasion he said he hoped to be an engineer someday, I decided I wanted to be an engineer, too. It was months later that I discovered to my chagrin that Terry's goal was not to drive a train!

As I got older, I naturally came to believe that real men must be mechanical. I pictured being a competent husband as one who any day could return home, put on his belt of tools and go around the house fixing or building things.

Consequently, after Jackie and I were married, I became determined to repair things, skillfully carrying out my manly duties as every husband should. Sadly, I would literally spend hours working on my car, only too often needing to call a friend to help me fix my fixing.

I unfortunately spent many of my early years of marriage *pretending* that I would one day be a mechanical husband, and like Superman swoop to Jackie's side bringing handyman-like assistance to every household need. *"I'll show my wife that I can be a competent husband,"* I thought to myself so many times.

Worse yet, much of the time my daydreaming about my proficient use of hammers, wrenches and screwdrivers stymied me from taking responsibility to see that my family's needs were met, mechanical or not. I would typically procrastinate when I knew a dripping faucet needed attention and I had no clue how to fix it. I would often stall by stating in a rather pious tone, "I just don't have the time to get to that right now, Jackie."

It was only when I began to understand the freedom I had, in spite of my deficiencies, to see that the mechanical problem was taken care of. Jackie never demanded that I fix or build anything. She was ministered to far more when I began to take responsibility for her needs showing that I truly cared about her.

Yes, we can change our behaviors, to develop and improve our abilities. Over the years, for example, I have enjoyed much more liberty to ask a neighbor or friend for assistance and then to learn how I might be able to solve the problem the next time. But I also grew to accept that I will never be a handy-man and that there are many jobs I don't ever need to tackle.

When we begin to require that we act a certain way or obtain a specific ability before we serve God, we strip away much of His power to use us in the lives of others.

Ironically, God with His wonderful sense of humor, has placed me next door to or across the street from numerous handymen, including the place we moved to here in Indiana several years ago.

Although they don't know it, these friends have been often used by God to help me face the fact that I am truly a mechanical klutz but my personhood and manhood are still intact. I could still be responsible and yet didn't have to become something I'm not.

To this day I'm now free to go to a neighbor, seek out their help and frankly admit that I'm not very good at those kinds of things. It's become okay to need their help. In fact, the fact that I need their assistance often opens the door to start or develop a relationship with that person.

My need can become the comfort they need to face the otherwise awkwardness of getting to know a stranger.

Some FEELING must change.

Have you ever felt sorry for an extremely depressed person? I have. Their drawn face and slumping shoulders can elicit a concerned response from the people around them. I have often wished that I could physically lift their spirits, but I also know it's not really up to me.

And yet depression (not the clinical kind) is often a safe place for people to hide. They have learned, even subconsciously, that when they are depressed, others cannot expect them to function normally. (I'll speak more about depression in chapter eleven.)

Others, even those not struggling with depression, require that their feelings toward a particular person must go away before they can change. *"If my mother just didn't make me so angry maybe I could relate to her for once,"* the embittered daughter mourns. *"If only I could feel comfortable with our new pastor,"* the longstanding elder sighs.

Unfortunately, our feelings for others may never change, especially if the other person stays the same! Nevertheless, those feelings have no right to control what we say and do or determine whether we live our lives for God or not!

Our demands that these changes happen are as realistic as requiring that our backyard suddenly become the Grand Canyon. We're waiting for fantasies that may never, ever come true. It's far more important to work on changing us and our responses.

What daydreams dominate your thinking and keep you ineffective and unproductive? What are you waiting for before you reach new heights? Are you dreaming that your spouse will one day be a new person before you confront their inappropriate actions?

Maybe you keep streaming in your mind a sad song about your father or mother's lack of acceptance of you, wishing that things could have been different?

It's interesting to note that Jesus told the woman at the well that if she was going to worship God, she must worship *in spirit and in truth*.

It's possible that your ability to worship God and get to know Him intimately has been hindered by a hope that will never happen.

Remember that God is a God of truth, not falsehood, reality not a false world of pretension. There's a better way. Two later chapters will talk about how to move from *someday to NOW*. But there's one more fuel you need to ponder.

Things To Think About In Chapter Five

List several potential relationship fantasies that you're realizing may never occur.

What do you do to dull the pain of those fantasies not becoming realities?

How has waiting on them kept you from growing or changing?

What new thoughts might you need to be thinking that will take the influence of those fantasies away?

THE FUEL OF FRENZY
CHAPTER 6

"While I am busy with little things, I am not required to do greater things." Francis De Sales

Some years ago, a Tacoma, Washington newspaper carried the story of Tattoo the basset hound. Tattoo didn't intend to go for an evening run, but when his owner shut the dog's leash in the car door and took off for a drive with Tattoo still outside the vehicle, little Tattoo had no choice!

Thankfully, motorcycle officer Terry Filbert noticed a passing vehicle with something dragging behind it.

Tattoo was *"picking up his feet and putting them down as fast as he could,"* the officer later stated. He chased the car to a stop and the dog was rescued but not before he had reached a speed of twenty to twenty-five miles an hour, rolling over several times.

Ouch! How often do we feel like poor Tattoo, trying to keep up with speeding cars in our lives, wondering when we'll give out because things are moving way too fast? Have you noticed the speeding drivers on our roads these days? Are you one of them, endangering yourself and others because you just have to get there now?

Anne Phillips crawls out of bed every morning at 5:45am, darkness shrouding the twinkling street lights in her modest, but comfortable subdivision. Two children,

Jennifer, age 4, and Jason, age 7, remain peacefully asleep while Anne scurries to shower and dress before she must wake them.

Husband, Don, has been up since 5:15 and while fixing his stylish tie whispers, *"Hi, honey,"* as she rushes towards the kitchen to prepare lunches. *"Oh, how I wish just one morning I could let the kids sleep,"* she mulls to herself as she plasters the last piece of baloney with mustard while laying it between two slices of rye bread.

As Don walks briskly into the kitchen for coffee, Anne remembers to tell him about Jason's soccer game at six that evening and to ask if he wouldn't mind picking up some sort of fast food to bring to the game. He replies, *"Sure, babe,"* gives her a quick kiss and is out the door for his forty-five-minute drive to the office.

Anne next heads to Jason's room and tenderly but urgently wakes him, nudging him towards the clothes she set out the night before that he will wear to school. Jennifer is always hard to wake up, but Anne finally succeeds, sort of, and helps her get dressed. The preschooler dozes off several times before Ann can finish the last button and comb her hair.

Breakfast during the week is almost always juice, cereal and toast. There isn't time for anything more or better. She hopes the chewable vitamin that she places next to their food will make up some of the nutritional deficiencies.

On cold days she tries to get the car warmed up ahead of time to provide some comfort during the trip to Sarah's house. Sarah, her best friend, watches the children until it's time for them to catch the school bus and then keeps them after school until Anne returns from work.

Today, Anne will work eight hours with a half hour lunch break, then drive to Sarah's to get the kids to take them to the soccer game. She'll return home around eight with Don in tow, prep the kids for bed and finally sit down in her favorite chair utterly exhausted, wishing that the next day were a Saturday.

But it won't be. She'll do the same thing all over again in just a few short hours.

The agenda won't be exactly the same but the exhaustion will be. Busyness will win out again. Frenzy will serve as the norm neatly disguised under the banner of, *"I'm trying to do what's best for my family."*

Weekends won't provide much respite either as housework, music lessons, sports tournaments, shopping and church activities take center stage. Anne won't feel like much of a mother or wife either, but will spend long hours as a taxi driver, Mother Teresa, public servant and weary disciple.

She and Don will have shared only a few sentences of conversation, the majority of their conversation describing details of the next place they needed to be or who was going to do what.

Most outside observers would say that Don and Anne have a solid marriage, but Anne certainly knows why their sexual relationship has become cordial at best and why she can't remember the last time the two of them just sat and talked or went on a date.

Even church has gradually become more of an obligation than a joy and when her cell phone rings she looks to see if the caller is a potential add-on to her schedule.

Whatever happened to time to have fun and be spontaneous? When will they find even a moment to teach their children spiritual truth, learn about the Bible and get outside and soak in the beauty of God's creation?

Somehow the amount of guilt they feel about those omissions doesn't solve the problem.

Of course, Anne has dreams and goals, lots of them: a vacation to Florida, a continuing education class, starting a women's Bible study, reading a book, sorting through old photos, traveling to see her aging parents and exercising. But life's demands are always the victor, as her world relentlessly loads one more brick onto her self-driven cart of expectations, obligations and commitments.

Do you know an Anne and Don? Are you either one? Does your lifestyle or that of your family sound familiar with only the names and places changed? Millions of families live in mayhem, convinced that there are no other options. You probably do, too.

But deep within you know there is more. You long to stop and enjoy your spouse, children, and extended family more. You wish that what you do to serve others could be savored longer and better planned. You have a passion to know God more deeply instead of whispering a prayer or two to him while you rocket through your day.

"Will I ever be able to take life in instead of give out all the time?" you lament. Is it any wonder that much of our joy and excitement is usually over the next hill or around the corner?

In fact, frenzy can have disastrous results. Brenda, an assistant principal at an Ohio middle school, was on her way to work on an early September morning when she said she realized it was too early to drop off her toddler. So, she stopped to buy doughnuts for colleagues at school.

Distracted by the change in her routine, she says she completely forgot her little two-year-old girl was sleeping in the back of the car. She unloaded the doughnuts and walked past Cecilia in the back seat on the driver's side a half dozen times.

Brenda parked her car and went into the school around 7 a.m. Eight hours later, the toddler was discovered by someone in the parking lot. Teachers frantically called 911 and attempted CPR. Cecilia died.

The temperature outside hovered around 100 degrees all day. Police say it could have reached 140 degrees inside the car. *"I don't know how you go on having done this to one of your kids and ever forgive yourself,"* the distraught mom said,

NOW!

her voice breaking as she slumped against the wall and answered questions.

But here's the most telling and tragic comment of all. *"I was just trying to be everything to everyone, and I failed my daughter."* This same scenario continues to repeat itself in spite of newer technology that can now warn parents that a child is still in the car.

"I was just trying to be everything to everyone." Every parent's nightmare, the loss of a child, occurred because a mother's life was too full, too pressured, too fixed on pleasing everyone around her.

A *USA Today* poll asked a group of mothers what they needed most. The most popular response? Thirty-two percent said *more time in their day.* In fact, time has become more precious to us all.

Recent surveys suggest that more than fifty percent of people now work more than twelve hours a day to get all their tasks done. More than half of people admit to worrying that they don't have enough time to spend with family and friends.

And only thirty-two percent of kids age nine to fourteen say they spend a lot of time with their parents. Sixty-three percent of kids that same age say, if granted one wish, they would want their mom or dad to have a job that gave them more time to do fun things together as a family.

The causes of our hectic pace

An increased number of options.

Individuals and families today have more choices than ever before. There is a virtual option explosion that continues to grow right before our eyes. And each new choice carries with it more potential ones to follow.

Kid's, for example, don't just choose to play basketball for a three or four-month season. They are often required to participate in pre-season camps, post-season workouts, summer clinics, traveling teams, off-season leagues and special conditioning sessions.

They play at 7:00am, after school, at night and even on Sundays. Similarly, schools don't just provide band and choir anymore. Now students have a similar smorgasbord of options from Jazz Band to Madrigals to the school musical to choose from or even be required to join.

Churches have also expanded their activity menus, offering the Christian consumer support groups, Bible studies, aerobics, drama teams, multiple choirs, different sites for worship, mission trips and discipleship options.

The choices aren't all bad and seem usually well-intended, but to some they also appear attractive, necessary and compelling. Even Starbucks' options offer customers over 100,000 ways just to get a specialty beverage!

And as blessed as we are having myriad choices for most things, we can also become addicted to them and more time gets stolen from us as we sort through all the possibilities. Consider the number of options you receive online, for example, after you simply research the purchase of one new item!

All sorts of companies contact you via ad, mail or phone with their *great idea* that is supposed to solve your problem. And there might be some excellent options there for you but you just can't make the time for any more.

Both spouses working.

Let's face it the two-parents working phenomenon has been here for a long time. The past fifty-plus years have witnessed a huge rise in the number of women in the paid work force, from fifteen percent of mothers of children aged six and under in 1950 to sixty-five percent today.

Three-quarters of mothers of children eighteen and under now work. Indeed, American women now make up nearly half of the American labor force.

And my point here is not to beat up on moms who work or to call us to return to the good old days. But we must face the fact that many children, like Anne's, are shuffled from babysitter to school to daycare, while parents (or a parent) are exhausted much of the time trying to meet all of life's demands.

Many a family's schedule would give the President's day a run for his money and they don't have his aides and assistants! Meals together are rare and any thoughts of family worship or spiritual learning together have become relics of the past.

Naturally, many factors enter a couple's decision to both work–needed funds, job choices, education, personal esteem and the like. Scores of families have both parents working to pay the bills. The question for our purposes here isn't whether both parents should work or not.

The truth is that many do. In fact, there are tens of thousands of families with only one spouse employed who are still over-committed and running ragged.

Unfortunately, when both partners work there is less time left for the essentials of healthy and biblical family living such as communication, personal time together and spiritual training. Instead well-meaning parents relegate the best things to future somedays when the kids are older, they go on vacation, someone works a different shift, summer arrives, the weekend comes or the house is finished.

And most of the time *someday never comes*. The tyranny of the urgent and the need for the extra income wins out most often leaving the potential for great memories and special moments behind.

Everybody's doing it!

Most of us have used this old line on our parents at some point in our lives. *"But mom, everyone's doing it!"* Or *"They're all going to the game, why can't I?"* However, the fact is that when it comes to being busy, everyone IS doing it! Some even enjoy and live for the attention they receive when others see how much they can pack into one week.

Attending all those games, running to the next rehearsal and having fun with all the other parents who do the same can provide its rush of exhilaration. We're exhausted, but in a way, it sort of feels good. We'd just be bored at home anyway, right?

For others, there is something compelling talking to others about our busyness. We get people's attention when we explain how bad our schedule has been this week. It feels good to have a story that is equally dramatic as our friend's tale about the rigors and challenges of everyday living.

Think about it. What would it be like if your neighbor told you about their busy, productive, exhausting week where each child was participating in several trendy and stimulating activities? You know, weekly ballet lessons, gymnastics, art class and Karate. Then they ask, "*So how was your week?*"

Would most of us be content to respond, "Well, I got to take Sarah to the dentist on Thursday. The rest of the week I just picked her up from school and we came home." Somehow your world would feel like a Chevy next to their Lexus.

When everyone seems to be living on the fast track it's not easy to drive through life at thirty miles an hour. And unfortunately, the world around us is not our ally in the battle. More than ever, schools pressure our children to be busy all the time, often with some overly ambitious teachers making it nearly impossible for a quality student to say "*no.*"

Years ago, our kids' school had a vocal organization that required involvement in at least two other music groups, both of which required out of school involvement. Students hardly know what a day off is any more with most vacations now open season for special rehearsals, workouts, competitions and the like.

Our son Tim was a trumpet player in high school, a quite good musician, if I don't say so myself! His band won numerous competitions and the students developed a healthy sense of pride and accomplishment because they worked appropriately hard. My wife and I are thankful for the commitment of their leaders to both excellence and giving the students a love for music.

However, consider the commitment they made to band, just one of several activities for most students: two weeks of sectional rehearsals in June, ten days of camp in August (seven and a half hours a day), seven am rehearsals during school, two evening rehearsals a week and a Tuesday sectional after school. That's the requirement for one student for one activity!

But it's hard as a parent to say, *"Enough is enough,"* isn't it? And yet there are more important things than being busy every moment of every day.

Recently I saw a national news story about a community in New Jersey that planned a free night for their town. It took them nine months to pull it off but the churches, schools and community organizations all agreed to not schedule anything on one evening.

What a great idea, but how sad that it had to be scheduled. None of us wants our child to be considered a nerd or geek because he or she won't take part in the activity merry-go-round. We certainly want our children to have the opportunities other young people have.

But when I was a pastor I also noticed the debilitating effects of busyness on people's ability to be quiet before God and to focus on Him in worship services. Silence has somehow become a vanishing value along with contemplation and meditation.

I remember attending another church where I found the worship lively and exciting but wondered after forty minutes of non-stop singing when we were ever going to simply be still before the Lord. It never happened.

Lack of specific priorities

Jackie and I have made a regular practice of getting away by ourselves to review the past twelve months and look ahead at the next year or two. I am immensely grateful for the insights, poignant reminders and challenges we have encountered during these mini-vacations. In fact, my being a pastor today is in part a result of one of those breaks from our routine.

The most important component of our time together, however, was re-visiting the things that we would die for and then re-committing ourselves to do whatever it takes that year to keep those priorities central. We know that without intentionality we will drift anywhere our culture's currents take us.

This list will of course differ from yours, but here are priorities we tried to cling to early on in our marriage and then when children joined our home:

Spiritually training our kids
Enjoying meals together on a regular basis
Regular church attendance, involvement and service
Trips together as a couple and family
Family traditions
Supporting one another's accomplishments
Regular family nights
Rest and relaxation

We found that we would use this list or one like it to guide where and how we drew the line on more demands of our time. If our kids, for example, both wanted to be involved in activities that would mean we could rarely eat meals together or ever attend one another's functions, we either found different activities or didn't participate.

If any of us were to be offered a job keeping us from worship together on Sunday, even before I was a pastor, we didn't accept the opportunity. Priorities help us to manage our time and not allow time to manage us!

You see, it's not just busyness or limited time that's the problem. We are all busy and none of us gets more than twenty-four hours. Ephesians 5: 15, 16 says it well, *"Be very careful then, how you live—not as unwise, but as wise, making the most of every opportunity, because the days are evil."*

Setting priorities and determining what things will actually drive how we live are *our responsibility.* As many of you know, Pastor Rick Warren wrote an extremely popular book called *The Purpose Driven Life* entirely devoted to this idea. It's still worth your reading or a re-read.

Making the most of our time

Without getting you to act or change merely because of guilt, let me list here some of *God's explicit challenges* and requirements that He makes of every Christ follower. He gives these to us not to add extra burdens to an already full life, but to make sure that we find joy, happiness and fulfillment when we live out what we were really meant to be.

"Go therefore and make disciples of all nations . . . " (Matthew 28:18) I wonder if this commandment has been forgotten in many homes, blurred out by the demands life places on us every day. It's not merely the task of the corporate church to answer this call. Jesus spoke these words to His closest followers before the church was even in existence.

Somehow the ebb and flow, pace and direction of our lives must reflect a commitment and impassioned desire to do our part in this *Great Commission.* The training and discipling of our families (see the next point), sharing our stories with those who do not know Christ and serving our world in Jesus' name will take their rightful role in our schedules.

Imagine that you have been offered the rather special privilege of spending $86,000 every day, funds placed in your bank account every morning. Your task is to use every dollar with only one condition. You must dole it out that day. Nothing can be carried over to the next day. Sounds like a fun job, doesn't it?

In reality, we have been given a similar commodity of 86,000 seconds. And not one second carries over to the next day. We all have the same amount of time to do the things that matter but that time will speed by. We must manage it and live a life that includes reproducing other disciples.

We must, however, become intentional about how we function each day. We have to remain passionate about lost people who need someone to show them where life and meaning can be found.

Don't let the things the world has told us are urgent take the place of those that are most important like reaching and loving those who don't know Christ.

"And these words which I am commanding you today . . . you shall teach them diligently to your sons." (Deuteronomy 6: 6,7) I worked in a Christian high school for fifteen years and look back on that season of my life with fond memories.

However, during those years I saw a trend that was particularly disturbing. It was the gradual movement of Christian parents away from the spiritual training of their own children. And in talking to Christian educators more recently I am confident that this tendency continues today.

Although few parents ever said it out loud, I often hear the unmistakable message, *"Listen, I am counting on you to train my kids, to teach them the Bible, to help them apply it to everyday life and to get them to act accordingly. My wife and I are paying big money here to have our kids in this school so don't screw it up!"*

Yes, many moms and dads desired the right results but were often unwilling to accept even minimal responsibility to train their offspring to live godly lives. In fact, it's not surprising that churches all across our country are experiencing a deep decline in the amount of Bible knowledge both kids and adults have acquired.

Only thirty-five percent of teens read the Bible each week, not including when they were in church. But even more shocking is that only nine percent of born-again teens believe in moral absolutes and just four percent of the non-born-again teens believe in them.

Weekend children and youth leaders often report lines of cars dropping the kids off at church while mom and dad head off to breakfast. Larger churches offer more and more alternatives for the family while unintentionally encouraging many parents to guiltlessly abdicate their roles as spiritual trainers willing to simply let the church do it.

Yes, spiritual training does take time and effort. As noted earlier, the Old Testament book of Deuteronomy speaks powerfully about the important role parents play in the ongoing and natural spiritual training we must do for our children.

Here is the larger context: *"And these words which I am commanding you today, shall be on your heart, and you shall teach them when you sit in your house and when you walk by the way and when you lie down and when you rise up." (Deuteronomy 6:6,7)* But we must have time WITH our families if we are going to have any spiritual impact ON them in the first place.

Here are some challenging, yet important questions we must ask ourselves on a regular basis: When is the last time our family or we as a couple had devotions, family worship, prayed together or talked about what God is doing in our lives? Dad, when have you specifically taught your wife or child a principle or concept from the Bible?

My hunch is that many of us want to meet this challenge but we sometimes don't know how and more often simply do not have the time.

When our son Tim was in high school, I decided I needed to do something more specific with him even though his personal schedule and number of activities were increasing like most kids his age. So, we developed *D.A.D.* (Discussion and Development) nights.

About once a week we met together to talk plus give me an opportunity to build other spiritual truths into his heart and life. Sure, there were weeks when we couldn't meet and I certainly didn't do it all perfectly.

However, I was struck by the fact that I only had a few years left when he would still be in my home and where I could influence his learning about things eternal. God was clearly reminding me that I was to be his chief spiritual teacher.

Each week I prepared a doubled-sided page for him to keep and us to discuss. One side consisted of some sort of biblical content and some applications that could come from it. The other side included a practical living lesson about life in general.

My goal was that when we finished, he would have a notebook filled with life-sustaining, life-enriching truth that would impact him the rest of his life, all things he had learned from his dad. While it wasn't a stellar effort, I am so thankful for those months God gave us together.

There may be no greater challenge and no more rewarding endeavor a Christian parent can embrace than to teach their kids God's truth. The Bible is explicit that we as parents, not the church, are to be the prime instructors for our children when it comes to spiritual things. The added advantage we have is that they can also watch us model our faith in everyday life!

In fact, since the founding of Israel, God has challenged His people with the huge task of passing on their faith to future generations. "*He decreed statutes for Jacob and established the law in Israel, which he commanded our forefathers to teach their children so the next generation would know them, even the children yet to be born and they in turn would teach their children."* (Psalm 78: 5-8)

God never considered the spiritual training of children optional. It's a COMMAND. And let's not buy into the notion that quality time makes up for quantity time. A classic *Doonesbury* cartoon tells the real story. During the course of a radio interview with "Mark," a man who has written a book on child-rearing is asked about his concept of quality time.

His response says it all, *"For sure, Mark, quality time is the kind of time you spend with your kids if you're really too pressed to give them the more traditional quantity time."*

That is so right. We've been tricked into believing that we can cram more love, interest, caring and involvement into a smaller space and our children won't see the difference. The problem is that younger children can't mentally discern the difference between quantity and quality anyway.

Their abstract thinking skills are not developed enough to make the distinction. A five-year-old, for example, won't be saying, *"You know mom, we didn't have much time together today but it sure was rich!"*

Parents, we have a mandate from God to instill through our teaching and modeling *"The praiseworthy deeds of the Lord, his power and the wonders he has done."* And if a frenetic lifestyle stands in the way, then something needs to change.

"But speaking the truth in love, we are to grow up into Him who is the Head, even Christ." (Ephesians 4:15) *We were made to mature, to grow, to bear fruit, to become like Jesus. "So then just as you received Christ Jesus as Lord, continue to live in Him."* (Colossians 2:6) As I said in an earlier chapter, following Christ is a step by step process. *It's a walk.*

The Christian life was never intended to be a static existence. Jesus modeled a life that was vibrant, purposeful and in intimate relationship with the Father. It is not coincidental that Scripture repeatedly describes our relationship with God as a parent and child.

"Because you are sons, God has sent the Spirit of His Son into our hearts, the Spirit who calls out, 'Abba, Father.' (Galatians 4:6) "Abba" can most accurately be translated, "Daddy."

As Christ followers we are children of God and normal children grow. They need to mature because they were designed that way. But to truly be healthy and robust in our faith relationship we must eat and care for ourselves just as we do physically.

For some of us who are new to our faith, eating may involve only consuming spiritual baby food while others will eat steak. The important thing is that we eat. *"Like newborn babies, crave spiritual milk, that by it you may grow up in your salvation."* (1 Peter 2:2)

Some of us in our fast track world may wonder why our inner lives are tepid and bland even though we may have scores of spiritual pursuits and opportunities around us. The problem may very well be spiritual malnutrition because spiritual food isn't being ingested on a regular basis and as a result our nourishment suffers.

Our spiritual energy becomes drained and passion for Christ-like living is diminished. What we need, at least in part, is the nutrition of the Bible, God's truths, to replenish our souls, to sink deeply into our soul and sustain us every day. We need these meetings with God that come through exposure to His speaking in the Scriptures. More on that later.

A Better Way

Wonder with me whether the demands on your time have literally sapped the richness that God wants you to enjoy in your relationship with Him? Maybe your busyness is really a way to avoid a face to face encounter with God. Robert Gates in *The Tyranny of Time* writes:

"Most people have a deeply rooted dread of time and are afraid to look in its face. That is why they are constantly endeavoring to forget themselves, ignore the past and avoid looking into the future."

As the Bible reminds us over and over again, those who turn away from God will find that their works are vain and that they exhaust themselves for nothing. This is what we see taking place before our eyes."

If you're hiding behind the frenzy of your schedule, you may be like Adam and Eve, hiding behind the good bushes God made. You're afraid to encounter Him while exposed, naked and sinful. But you see the goal of the Christian life must never be to only know about God, but rather to know him intimately. And knowing God takes time.

Gary Thomas in Authentic Faith says, *"In spite of our obsession with instant results, we serve a God whose calendar moves by millennia, not minutes, and who thinks in terms of generations, not seasons. Unless we understand this about God . . . we will never understand his ways with us."*

Israel was chastised by Jeremiah for this very reason: *"'You live in the midst of deception; In their deceit they refuse to acknowledge Me, declares the Lord.'" (Jeremiah 9:6)*

But he later writes under the direction of God's Holy Spirit, *"But let him who boasts boast of this that he understands and knows me, that I am the Lord who exercises kindness, justice, and righteousness on earth." (Jeremiah 9:24)* We have but seventy or so years on this earth and they pass by all too quickly.

We must start NOW to examine the time we have left and, with God's help, determine where our focus will be today until we die. Will our lives reflect only ourselves and our wishes or will they be a model of God's purposes and plans? The Apostle Paul's challenge was clear. *"I want to know Christ." (Philippians 3:10)*

Will you commit to a life filled with intimate encounters with the God, determined to know Christ better and better? That's the better way. Or will you continue to wait for someday when your schedule is freer? This is the time to say, *"No more someday living for me, no more excuses."* My time is going to allow me (us) to live for Jesus NOW!

Of course, no one will be able to sit around all day and meditate on God and the meaning of life. But He never planned for us to do that! Even in Heaven we will be serving, not just sitting! Revelation 22:3 says, *"And his servants will serve him."*

But it's essential that we take control of the moments God has given us and afford ourselves the time necessary to make changes, to ponder our futures and begin to live out our purposes.

In the next two chapters, I'll discuss how we can actually move from life in the someday to living NOW. It's time to move on to having more significant moments and experiences.

Read on to find out how.

Things to Think About in Chapter 6

Where do you have margin, extra space and time in your life? If you don't have any, why not?

What could you give up or not do anymore so that your life isn't so frenzied and busy?

What would you do with that extra time if you had it?

What new goals and plans is God speaking to you about?

SOMEDAY TO NOW-PART 1
CHAPTER 7

"One day you will wonder what was so important that you put off doing the most important things. Someday can be a thief in the night."
Deborah Brown

Change is rarely easy or spontaneous. The comfort of long-held habits and well-rehearsed strategies, even those which are ultimately unfulfilling and damaging, makes our attempts at life modification challenging at best.

Churches have some of their most destructive arguments and splits over seemingly simple and relatively unimportant changes – the church name, style of worship, the times for the weekend services and the color of the walls.

Every year millions of New Year's resolutions fade away into the mist of habit, comfort and someday, to remain in hibernation for at least 365 more days. To continue a diet, exercise program, reading plan or savings strategy is hard enough. But altering key components in the way we think and live is nearly impossible without outside help!

In fact, if we're going to move from living in the *someday* to being people of NOW, change must occur in our attitudes, thinking and lifestyle. We must become *fundamentally different*, not merely through an altered exterior, but as the result of reshaped minds.

Paul speaks about this process in Romans 12: 1,2, *"I urge you, brothers, in view of God's mercy, to offer your bodies as living sacrifices, holy and pleasing to God–this is your spiritual act of worship.*

Do not conform to this world, but be transformed by the renewing of your mind. Then you will be able to test and approve what God's will is–his good, pleasing and perfect will."

God also reminds us through King David that He desires more than just an external facelift. Consider Psalm 51: 16-17, *"You do not delight in sacrifice, or I would bring it. You do not take pleasure in burnt offerings. The sacrifices of God are a broken spirit: a broken and contrite heart, O God, you will not despise."*

Resistance to Significant Change

Why is it that we are so reluctant to amending our lifestyles? We sit in our worship services, at times deeply moved and challenged by the Word and the Spirit, yet find it so hard to break free from our everyday ways of life. We are well aware of our debilitating habits and unhealthy attitudes, and yet give into the inertia of our lives much of the time.

We may read helpful books and confidently say, *"Yes! This is what I needed to hear and I WILL be different."* But, even after tearful and remorse-filled commitments to turn unhealthy ways into godly obedience, our passions revert back to what we did yesterday. Why is that?

Change is often uncomfortable.

Some years ago, we visited our married daughter, Amy and her husband, David, in China where they were teaching in a Christian international school. We had an incredible time and enjoyed seeing how God was using them in such profound ways.

During our stay we took a six-hour train ride to Beijing to see some of the sites, including the Great Wall.

However, on our trip back to their city we could only secure tickets on an overnight train, a journey of seven or eight hours.

I knew this might be a long night when after purchasing the tickets we were directed to a large room teeming with people waiting for our train. We found a few seats and began to sweat profusely because of the heat and humidity. Several hours later, we were able to head through our gate down to the train , enjoying a brief encounter with a cool breeze and fresher air.

But my son-in-law and I soon found our berth, receiving the top of three tiny sleeping areas on either side of a small aisle. Jackie and Amy were in a completely different car. To get to our bunk located eighteen or so inches from the ceiling, we had to climb up the side of the doorway! With both of us six-feet tall or more, that small space was cozy to say the least. I've had MRI's where I had more room!

As I organized my sheet and pillow, bracing my feet against my luggage at the foot of the bed, my mind began to wander. For a time, I smiled as I thought about how incredibly privileged we were to be spending this time with our *kids* in a once-in-a-lifetime experience. But soon I was pondering the comforts of home and how little sleep I was likely going to get that night.

Sometime in the wee hours of the night I was going to have to climb back down in the dark to use the bathroom, essentially a little hole in the floor surrounded by metal walls and a door. While this discomfort was only temporary my mind still wondered if we had made the right decision taking the train.

Maybe we should have flown? Why couldn't we take the fast train? Won't it be great to be back home in the U.S?

In fact, many people will even endure the worst discomfort to keep from experiencing the anticipated trauma of something new. I think of Sandy whose husband verbally and physically abused her, periodically ran off with the children on a whim and demanded that she wait on him hand and foot while he sat in front of the television.

I asked her one day, *"Sandy, why do you stay? Why do you put up with him?"* Her response was *surprising but typical, "I couldn't stand to be alone. At least with him I know what he will do and how to handle it."*

Change is usually hard work.

We have to concentrate intently and expend large amounts of energy to master something new. Do you remember when you first learned to ride your two-wheeler? Those initial few times around the block required constant focused attention on balance, direction and speed to keep you from tumbling to the ground.

And although you were thrilled with your progress, the butterflies still swarmed in your stomach as you maneuvered past those driveways and sidewalks you first conquered.

Your eyes busily scanned the street as your hands and arms rocked back and forth, barely sustaining your equilibrium. Nevertheless, it wasn't long before your nervousness eased into a comfortable anxiety and riding became much more joyful and exciting.

Unfortunately, in a society where speed is paramount in everything from computers to food preparation to shopping online, the hard work required for sustained change is unattractive to the majority of people.

Yet most of us would admit that the greatest accomplishments are those that require the most time, discipline and determination to achieve. It's hard not to be amazed at the athleticism of a professional basketball player, the magnificent dexterity of a concert pianist or the intrigue of a well-written drama.

Think about Michael Phelps, perhaps the greatest swimmer of all-time. His success took decades to achieve.

And yet he was also still swimming to win even during his final Olympic swim.

I am a golfer. Well, I like to play anyway. Once a friend of mine and I traveled to a nearby city to watch a practice round for the PGA Tournament, one of golf's majors each year. We had great fun, especially since during practice rounds the players are more relaxed, sign autographs, and actually talk to the fans.

However, my companion and I noticed one thing in particular. These were some of the best golfers in the world and yet they still put in an eight-hour day of practice! Most of the pros began by putting hundreds of balls from varying distances on a practice green.

Then they would walk over to the driving range with their coach and hit scores of balls with each iron and wood (metal). Soon they would go and play their practice round, many times hitting several balls from certain places on the fairway or bunker.

After the round they would head back to the range to hit clubs that had given them some problems during the round. Finally, they would go back and putt some more. Most of these golfers hit more balls in a week than the average golfer hits in a whole summer!

They know that even the smallest changes needed for them to improve their game will require tedious hours of plain old hard work. Our significant changes will require no less.

Change means taking responsibility for our actions

If you ever read the classic cartoon feature, *The Family Circle*, you no doubt recall the little ghosts who would appear over the heads of the children. These apparitions generally come on the scene when one of the parents would ask a question of the kids about who was at fault for some misbehavior.

NOW!

"Someone has been in the cookie jar," the mother exclaims. Suddenly, suspended in the air above every child is one of these little white creatures, each displaying the words, *Not Me,* prominently printed on their chests.

Similarly, most of us call on the *Not Me* ghost when we face the exposure of our own selfishness. As long as there is someone or something else to blame, the attention rarely needs to turn to us! And most of us have had a lot of practice with this maneuver, haven't we?

As children we often responded, *"He did it!"* Or *"It's her fault!"* As teens we switched to the line, *"But everyone else was doing it so why can't I?"*

When Adam, of Garden of Eden fame, was asked by God, *"Have you eaten from the tree which I command you not to eat from?"* he blamed Eve and God! *"The woman you put here with me—she gave me some fruit from the tree, and I ate it."* (*Genesis 3:11,12*)

You see, blaming provides us the opportunity to NOT live as we should. We believe the problem is the actions or problems of others so we don't have to own our part.

Consider again the non-clinically depressed person. She can easily ask, *"How can people expect me to function normally? Don't they know I'm depressed?"* The teenager still angry at his parents can continue to fail in school, get in trouble with the law and hang with unhelpful friends because in his mind his parents are the ones who messed him up.

The emotionally crippled adult child of an abusive parent may choose to remain a victim, appealing to her dysfunctional childhood as the barrier that keeps her from moving forward. In reality, she may be saying, *"I don't want to risk getting hurt again when I try to live normally in the real world."*

People who actually begin to change, moving from *someday* to NOW, must face their own part of the problem even though others may have wronged them in the past.

They must take responsibility for their own actions in the here and now.

God has not forgotten our past hurts! However, He has graciously given us the freedom, through Christ's death and resurrection, to move forward as valued individuals, having forgiven us of our attempts to protect ourselves from more pain.

Blaming others must start to leave our thinking and responsible choosing must gradually take its place. This is where God's power to help us forgive others is so essential. By forgiving others we are not endorsing their actions against us or forgetting what they did to hurt us.

In fact, remembering the sins others hold against us actually enriches and deepens our forgiveness. People of NOW will have to become people who forgive. I'll say more on this in the next chapter.

Change often hurts.

Discomfort is one thing but pain is way worse. At the dentist, having cotton in your mouth is uncomfortable and drilling causes pain. Early on in my musical training my teacher recognized that I had learned to avoid using the little finger on my left hand. The "pinky" is typically the weakest and I had simply learned to play without it.

My astute teacher knew, however, that playing without that one digit would seriously hamper my abilities in the future so he insisted that I begin exercises to develop its use.

The next few months were torture in my mind. I considered quitting many times, tearfully asking my mom and dad if I could end my lessons. Thankfully, my wise parents would usually say, *"Sure, Gary, you can quit – over our dead bodies! We didn't spend all this money for lessons so you could stop when it got hard."* They knew as well as I did that I must endure the pain of change.

For some, change will feel much like the loss of a loved one where old habits and ways of thinking will have to be grieved. Anger, deep sorrow, feelings of abandonment and betrayal will need to be processed, shared with God and a friend or counselor. Some have found journaling to be especially helpful during this process.

The point is: *pain must not be allowed to be a roadblock for the changes* we know God desires in us or that will move us forward as a person. I don't know of any surgery that doesn't require some pain. Nonetheless, surgery is usually for our best, designed to bring healing and better health in the long run.

In the same way we need to let God perform his surgery on us even though it may hurt for a while. We may feel as though God has left us and doesn't care. But He will still be there. Sometimes in his silence He is also reminding us that He is the ONLY answer, the ONLY one we serve, the ONLY one worth living for.

Change requires that we quit focusing on ourselves.

Gary Thomas in Authentic Faith also writes, *"Christians who let their weaknesses and inadequacies hold them back are just as self-focused as are believers who use their strengths to build self-glorifying kingdoms. When will we learn that it's not about us?"*

We must embrace the fact that so much of our motivation to stay where we are is because of self-protection.

Authentic change requires giving up our control and placing our hopes, dreams and future into the arms of a loving, passionate God who longs to see us be all we were intended to be. The first line of Rick Warren's *Purpose Driven Life* says it all, *"It's not about you."*

Adam and Eve were afraid because they'd been exposed. We have a tendency to live with our fear today of *being naked* before God when He wants to help us make progress just as we are.

The importance of walking

In chapter four, I reminded us of the Bible's regular use of the word *walk* to describe how the Christian functions. So, let's dig a little deeper. From mankind's earliest days the term walking has been associated with godly living. Genesis 5:24 says, *"Enoch walked with God."* Apparently, this was not always so according to verses twenty-one and twenty-two.

"When Enoch had lived sixty-five years, he became the father of Methuselah. And after he became the father of Methuselah Enoch walked with God."

The people of Israel heard similar words as they prepared to enter the Promised Land: *"Observe the commands of the LORD your God walking in his ways and revering him."* (Deuteronomy 8:6) In the New Testament the concept of walking is further refined as believers had Jesus Christ upon whom they could model their Christian walk, prompting John to write, *"Whoever claims to live in him must walk as Jesus did."* (I John 2:6)

As I mentioned earlier, there are several walks highlighted in the New Testament, giving us a multi-faceted perspective on walking as Jesus walked.

Walking is done, however, in the *here and now*. We may have prepared well, walked long or short distances or faced numerous challenges during childhood. Nevertheless, today we can only walk in the present. Thinking about the final mile we must cover or moaning about our poor performance yesterday or last year will do us little good now.

If we are going to make progress, we must realize that the only actions and attitudes we can control are those we manage in the moment.

In contrast, paralysis sets in when Christians try to live in the past or the future. Life resorts to the status quo when thoughts like, *"I've never been able to . . . ,"* *"If only my husband wouldn't have . . . ,"* or *"If I can just . . ."* permeate our thinking and corresponding actions. We often illustrate this in our conversations. It's easy to say to a spouse, *"You never listen to me!"* or to a child, *"You always have to do things your way."*

Do you hear the echoes of the past and predictions for the future in those statements? People of NOW learn to change those comments to, *"Right now I'm irritated because it seems like you're not listening to me,"* or, *"I'm upset because it sounds like you aren't open at the moment to any other ideas except your own."*

People of NOW realize they can courageously take steps of obedience, faithfulness and productivity in the present, no matter what others say and do.

James addressed this idea when he said: *"Come now, you who say, 'Today or tomorrow we shall go to such and such a city, and spend a year there and engage in business and make a profit. Yet you do not know what your life will be like tomorrow . . . . Instead, you ought to say, 'If the Lord wills, we shall live and also do this or that . . . Therefore, to one who knows the right thing to do, and does not do it, to him it is sin. (James 4: 13-17)*

James is speaking of more than the power of positive thinking here. He is referring to the ability we have in Christ to choose to move forward based on God's power working through the abilities and circumstances we face today.

As an amateur, but experienced mountain fanatic, I know there are no shortcuts on a long hike or climb. Every step must be taken. Some are easy, some are challenging but they remain steps and you can't skip any.

In fact, I never climb a mountain that someone can drive up or summit by cog railroad. I want to talk to people on the summit who got there the same way I did, one step at a time.

Interestingly, many *Someday Syndromers* are overwhelmed before they start because they're looking at the top of the mountain so to speak. They only see the whole task or change not the parts and reaching the top seems like too much for them.

My son Tim and I looked at and studied *Longs Peak* for days before we climbed it, examining it from every possible view, wondering what it would be like standing on the summit, trying to anticipate the inherent dangers for novices like ourselves. But eventually we had to go to the trailhead and get started. (Remember, read *Never Quit Climbing* for details).

And we did. We began walking even though we knew we had sixteen miles ahead of us.

Remember our earlier discussion of Deuteronomy 7? Let's review verse 22 again, *"The Lord your God will drive out those nations before you little by little. You will not be able to eliminate them all at once, or the wild animals will multiply around you."*

You see it was not God who couldn't handle the operation all at once. It was the people who had the limitations. In the same way, God accepts that change for us may come slowly, *little by little,* that it's walking, not jumping, that gets us to the next place most effectively.

Sometimes the quick answer isn't the best answer but rather a damaging one!

The kinds of walking we must do

Remember, the Bible describes the Christian walk as multi-faceted, like a diamond that sparkles in different ways depending upon how you look at it. Our walks could be compared to a finely woven tapestry, each component playing a different role on our journey.

However, to help us deepen our understanding I want to look at the various walks in the order we tend to understand them as we mature in Christ. While Paul does talk about our also *running the race,* the Christian life is still a long hike with each dynamic below a critical one.

Some translations translate these as *live,* but *walk or trek* is definitely the more accurate rendering.

We walk in faith.

"For we walk by faith, not by sight." (II Corinthians 5:7) Faith in what? Certainly, our faith must ultimately be focused on God, that He truly exists, that He loves us unconditionally and continues to reveal Himself to us today. But we must also believe Him for two very vital things: One, that *His love is the love we long for* in others and things and two, *In God's eyes we do matter.*

Although we may not always feel loved or important (and much of the world around us reminds us that we are neither), we have to take first steps of growth and movement based on these two truths.

Al and Christi came to see me as newlyweds of eight or nine months, incredibly hurt by their many recent fights.

Al would head for his favorite hobby, building remote control vehicles, as soon as the criticism and bickering began. As a result, Christi would become upset because she wanted to talk to Al and work through their issues. But Al would always clam up and head for his world of models in the garage.

As we talked, Al began to explain how as a kid he was constantly teased for being a fat, little boy. He wanted to matter so desperately to his friends, but they rarely cooperated. Instead their merciless taunting enlarged the ache in Al's heart. He soon started avoiding criticism at all costs. If Al could please people or avoid the hurt of rejection he would do it somehow.

And being alone seemed to work well most of the time. Each day after school he would be drawn to his safe world of models, secure in this numbing oasis from the realities of life at school. The warmth of his own model-building competence seemed to soothe the wounds experienced during the day from his insensitive and cruel peers.

When Al married, it was only too easy to follow the same path when Christi was unhappy with him. He feared being cast again as an incompetent jerk, this time in front of someone who meant the world to him!

Interestingly, Al and Christi had concluded that their problem was how to communicate and asked for some help in relating more effectively to one another. And yes, they did need some assistance in how to deeply and effectively connect with each other. But to merely offer them a few communication techniques would have missed their deeper needs by a mile!

Al had to come to grips with who he was in Christ, that he was loved, accepted and worthwhile in spite of his past. He had been living for far too long with a giant flat-screen picture of Al, the little fat boy, who couldn't bear being rejected again.

As a result, Christi's dissatisfaction over any part of their household or relationship flashed into his consciousness as, *"Al is a failure. Al is a reject. Al is worthless."*

Just as he did as a child, Al retreated to his safe place of building models. Change for Al, however, did not begin by somehow resisting his urge or desire to build a fancy plastic airplane. Al's first need was to begin to let God change his image of himself and then, by faith, begin to live as though he really does look differently to God. Change was slow, but then so is walking.

Initially, Al had to practice just sitting in one place, intently listening to Christi's frustrations or concerns and then respond to her, *"It sounds like you feel really about* _____. *Tell me more."* Staying there at first and not running to his place of comfort was torturous for him, but he learned that he would survive and that he had moved toward his wife instead of running.

He began to understand that Christi's unhappiness, even if it concerned him, would not deplete his capacities as a man or a person. He was free to lovingly approach his wife in humble strength, confident that God could now use him to meet her needs.

He was walking by faith, a powerful confidence that God would not leave him or forsake him. It was the faith that God had placed in him when He trusted Christ. Faith that his personhood was still intact no matter how much he had failed or how poorly the world around him was functioning. Al was becoming a man of NOW by walking in faith!

Walk in the light

As we begin to take a few toddler-like steps, we do find some success and exhilaration, though at times we are still terrorized in the process. Nonetheless, we discover that the light begins to turn on about how Christ really does change us.

You don't have to be a physicist to know that light serves several basic purposes. For example, it helps us to see our way so we won't stumble in the darkness. Yet sadly, thousands of people are literally groping their way through life, tripping over the shadows of their past along with myriad *someday* hopes and demands that may never materialize.

But as we begin to see God's unfailing love for us, we discover a different path, one that has been there all along. God's light doesn't allow us to see the trail very far ahead. Instead, his light is more like that of a flashlight in the woods, only illuminating enough of the path for us to take the next few steps.

However, that will suffice because we walk by faith. We are at liberty to enjoy the next few paces rather than bemoan the fact that our journey will be a slow one.

John said, *"If we walk in the light as He himself is in the light, we have fellowship with one another, and the blood of Jesus*

His Son cleanses us form all sin." (I John 1:9) Relationships with others can also deepen as we begin to see both the past and the present in the light of God's holiness, love and righteousness.

His light always shows situations, relationships and actions in the proper light, not what we wish it to be. It can show the smudges on the windows of our life that seem clean to us.

We walk in love

Walking in the light, however, prepares us best for the third dynamic of the Christian walk, walking in love. *"Therefore, be imitators of God, as beloved children. And walk in love, just as Christ also loved you, and gave Himself up for us, an offering and a sacrifice to God as a fragrant aroma. (Ephesians 5:2ff)*

You see most *Someday Syndromers* aren't very good lovers in the general sense. If you recall the three fuels I discussed in chapters four through six, you'll better understand what I mean.

The first fuel is *fear.* Fear undermines authentic relationship. I John 4:18 says it clearly, *"There is no fear in love; but perfect love casts out fear."* We avoid loving deeply and intimately because we fear rejection and abandonment.

To protect ourselves we keep many relationships on the surface, proper, calculated, business-like and strained at best. We wonder much of the time what will happen if we are ever found out for what we really are like inside.

The second fuel, *fantasy,* also diminishes our capacity to love deeply. When we only dream of more, we tend to love others conditionally, fantasizing about the changes in us or them that will help us love them someday.

Sadly, many Christians miss the joy of loving someone just the way they are right now including our spouses, children, friends, neighbors and associates. Instead we wait for the perfect scenario or just-right conditions before we can lose ourselves in relationship with them.

And obviously, the third fuel, *frenzy,* robs us of rich and meaningful connecting because we neither have the time nor take the time to enter into the life of another. Even if we did have margin, we don't have time to stay long enough to make much of a difference.

Walk in the Spirit

But as we begin to learn to live a NOW life, walking step by step in faith, light and love, we will begin to enjoy the fourth aspect of walking, walking in the Spirit. When we walk according to our own strength hoping that the future will somehow be better, we walk in the flesh, not in the power of God's Spirit. (Romans 8:3-5)

God's Holy Spirit is the One who continually helps us to transform our minds, (Romans 12:2), guides our thinking about where life can truly be found and enables us to put aside the thoughts that defeat us and keep us from change and meaningful service for God.

Listen to Paul's challenge in Romans 8: 5, 6, *"Those who live according to the sinful nature have their minds set on what that nature desires; but those who live in accordance with the Spirit have their minds set on what the Spirit desires. The mind of sinful man is death, but the mind controlled by the Spirit is life and peace."*

We will rarely enter the dark tunnels of our fears, hurts and pain without the power of God surging through us, compelling us onward to face the challenges and unknowns of living completely for our Father. We may talk about change or risk-taking for God but we will rarely experience either without the strength God's Spirit liberally offers us.

It's interesting, however, that the Bible speaks more about those things that hinder the Spirit than getting the Spirit. For example, Paul says in Ephesians, *"Be filled with the Spirit,"* (5:18) yet also says in Romans that all of us who are believers actually have the Spirit dwelling in us (Romans 8:9)

So, the question doesn't seem to be about how we get the Spirit as much as how do we become filled with the Spirit? The best answer may come from looking at the things that grieve the Spirit (Ephesians 4:30) and quench the Spirit (I Thessalonians 5:19).

In Ephesians 4:31 we are told that "*Bitterness, rage and anger, brawling and slander, along with every form of malice*" work against the power of the Spirit in us. A bitter person, for example, can only function in the past or the future, blaming the circumstances or individual who hurt them while anticipating how their life will continue to be less than it could have been.

She has never known the healing power of God which would allow her to lay down her inner pain, let go of the rage that demands others change and see herself as someone God loves.

As our bitterness and rage gradually subside, based on renewed thinking about who we are in Christ, we can become filled again with the Holy Spirit allowing Him to do great and mighty works in our lives including making significant changes and serving God meaningfully.

In fact, in I Thessalonians 5, quenching the Spirit is listed parallel to minimal prayer, not being thankful, not taking God's Word seriously and a lack of discernment.

People of NOW on the other hand are pray-ers, people who believe that God can work now. They praise God for what they have now believing and living as though what God says is really true. They choose not to flirt with temporary enticements to escape their hurt.

Walking a NOW kind of life will require faith, love, light and the Holy Spirit, each monitoring our steps, keeping us on the trail, even though it may be steep and difficult at times.

Spirit living may look and feel a little different to each of us as well. Some sense God's Spirit more when reading

Scripture while other hear God more in their thinking or quiet moments. There's no one right venue or means.

Identifying the path

In the next chapter I'll discuss several specific actions you can take to begin walking in the present and continue to do so the rest of your life. However, it's essential that you first decide where it is your walk is headed. Chances are there are important trails in your life that are sadly overgrown, barely detectable anymore because you've not hiked there for a long time, if ever.

Perhaps your trek needs to move you closer emotionally to your spouse. At present you rarely talk about your real feelings with each other and yet you long to have your life companion know and understand the real you.

You have hidden your struggles, pain, hopes and dreams for fear of ridicule, rejection or simply sounding silly. Hopefully you've decided that you will no longer wait for *someday* to seek deep intimacy again.

You must take a risk, perhaps only a small one at first, but a risky step nonetheless, towards your mate instead of retreating a protective distance away.

Others reading this may need to walk the way of forgiveness, choosing to no longer be bound by the uncontrolled actions of others. You will accept having to relinquish the control your lack of forgiveness gave you over your offender and his or her evil deeds.

The path to forgiveness is typically painful as memories of the hurts, abuses and words of death we experienced are once again stirred with in us. God may have to do some intensive surgery on our heart but it will be worth it.

Maybe you need to walk the path of deeper involvement with people in general. Out of fear you have lived much of your life cowering behind your self- or other-imposed feelings of inadequacy. You've too often refused to pursue relationships or to meaningfully connect with others in your everyday world. Or maybe God has been speaking to you about involvement in specialized ministry but you remain stymied and frozen, unwilling to risk trying.

There are hundreds of possible paths we might examine to help us become people of today and no longer be ruled by the *someday syndrome*. What directions do you need to pursue?

Ask the Holy Spirit right now to help you clarify the areas in your life that need significant change, relationships that still wait for reconciliation and serving opportunities you have feared to pursue.

List them in the spaces provided at the end of this chapter and then pray about each one. Ask God to reveal to you the reasons why you have resisted change, to forgive you and to give you the strength to begin taking some of the next steps listed in the following chapter.

Don't forget to consider the good that God placed in you when you first became His child. Picture that goodness growing and becoming something wonderful in you during the months and years ahead.

You can begin to live differently today. Start by deciding where to begin. In the next chapter you will read about some helpful equipment to take with you on your journey plus a few things to leave home!

Things to think about in Chapter 7

What are the segments of your life where you are most resistant to change? Why do you think that is?

What would be a first step for you to begin to be different in one or more of those areas?

What scares you the most about taking those first steps?

SOMEDAY TO NOW-PART 2
CHAPTER 8

"Enjoying God and involvement with others - in a word, improved
relationships - that's change!"
Larry Crabb

A re you ready to keep walking? I hope so. Walking
with Christ is one of the most freeing and
exciting things a believer can ever experience. Seeing the
Christian life as a step-by-step process releases us from
the pressure we place on ourselves to do it all.

Remember, moving forward isn't a short walk in the
park or a two-hour excursion to the mall. It's more like is
a marathon! Interruptions and major disappointments
shouldn't keep us from tackling life's most difficult paths.
We will experience fear, doubt, and even a desire to go
back just the way Israel did when things got rough.
Nonetheless, we can hold tightly to God being enough
for us.

Isaiah 40:9-31 gives great encouragement regarding
our lifelong journey:

*"He gives strength to the weary, and to him who lacks might He
increases power. Though youths grow weary and tired, and vigorous
young men stumble badly, Yet those who wait for the Lord will gain
new strength; They will mount up with wings like eagles, they will
run and not get tired, they will walk and not become weary."*

As you consider your path, note several things NOT to take with you. Leave these out as they'll simply weigh you down with things that hinder and hold you back.

What NOT to Pack in Your Spiritual Luggage

The temptation to blame others.

If you are ready to be change and quit waiting for tomorrow, as I alluded to earlier, you'll have to resist putting the onus on others. Of course, you can identify people who are culpable for some of the struggles you face like your parents, a boss, teachers, former classmates, your spouse, the pastor, the children, or dozens more candidates. There are actions some of them took and words some of them said which you can't control.

However, blaming others is comparable to handing your right to be healthy to another person on a silver platter. You might as well say, *"Here, take my life and let it be; when you decide to apologize and fix my problems, I'll be able to get on with life."* Blamers are usually, for all practical purposes, paralyzed.

If you find yourself condemning others, I suggest you write them a letter that they never get. Describe all the things you blame them for and why. Say it all. Then tell God you are ready to let go of their hold on you, that you forgive them for their wrong-doing, and that you won't carry it around any longer. Ask Him to help you move on NOW, live your life as God intended and walk free of their hold on you.

At some point, tear the letter up as a symbol of your choice to neutralize their power. As the song in the movie *Frozen* said, *"Let it go!"* If only it were that easy. Nonetheless, loosening our grip on certain things isn't impossible and is an important place to begin making changes.

Gary Sinclair

A demand for perfection.

In my counseling sessions, I often ask people to make a list of *"I musts"* and *"I must nots,"* things they require to be happy or okay. Most lists for *Someday Syndromers* have an, *"I must have things go perfectly,"* or some comparable statement on their list.

One goal of walking with Christ must be to become more like Him but not be equal to Him! I John 3:2, 3 says it well: *"Dear friends, now we are children of God, and what we will be has not yet been made known. But we know that, when He appears, we shall be like Him, because we shall see Him as He is. Everyone who has this hope in Him purifies himself, just as He is pure."*

It is highly inaccurate theology and certainly unrealistic to believe that we can be at God's level in this life. And yet, thousands of believers live in a fantasy world of personal perfection, seeking only gold medals and perfect tens. I recently watched the women's figure skating finals in the Olympics and almost every one of the medalists fell at least once in their program! *Diligence is godly; perfection is rare.*

Diane was a high school student who used to study for three or four hours just to take a quiz. Sadly, she attempted to commit suicide and I was asked to counsel with her during the weeks following. She got all A's and yet it soon became obvious that perfection was her goal. She didn't just desire good grades, she *demanded* them!

After several sessions discussing her compulsive studying and penchant for good grades, I suggested that she go home that night and not do any homework. At first, she couldn't believe her ears, hearing this strange challenge coming from an educator at the time!

And yet, even though it was difficult, a night of no homework helped Dane see that life would go on without her obsessive efforts to study for one evening. Her suicide attempt was the logical result of her lusting after a goal that was unreachable, but believing that it was essential for life!

In the same way, we don't need to panic when our walk of new relationships, changed behaviors, and godly service results in stumbles, falls, and disappointments. *Leave perfection home.*

What do you require be ideal these days? Your devotional life, your family, your church, your personal skills? To begin your walk, think of one area where perfection has a hold of you and literally try to NOT be perfect. And do it where someone else will likely notice!

For example, if you are a neat-freak at home, invite someone over but don't clean meticulously–leave a stack of magazines somewhere or a layer of dust on a counter top. See if you actually die or not. You won't. Begin to taste the freedom, during your panic, that you can enjoy to not live as a perfect ten.

Often, we get so engrossed in examining our inner life, peering microscopically at every little fault, that we do little changing on the outside. Listen to how C.S. Lewis in the *Screwtape Letters* has the novice demon give his nephew Wormwood advice:

"Keep his mind on the inner life. He thinks his conversion is something inside him and his attention is therefore chiefly turned at present to the states of his own mind . . . Encourage this. Keep his mind off the most elementary duties by directing it to the most advanced and spiritual ones. Aggravate that most useful characteristic, the horror and neglect of the obvious."

Excess weight.

A walk isn't much fun when we put too much in our pack. Hiking equipment such as shoes, backpacks, sleeping bags, etc. is designed using the lightest of materials. And yet many Christians carry loads of extra gear that is unnecessary. For example, they bring their bitterness. Bitter people don't let go of the pain that others have caused them.

They dwell on it. They view every thought, action, and statement of those who have hurt them as something to be made right or fixed.

Opportunities to experience joy become despair, while occasions for serving others turn into protection and manipulation. Words become biting and sarcastic while their thoughts fill with cynicism and doubt. Paul certainly understood bitterness and its accompanying symptoms when he wrote to the Ephesians: *"Get rid of all bitterness, rage and anger, brawling and slander along with every form of malice. (4:31)*

Shame.

I am confident that shame may weigh us down more than anything. Shame is more than just guilt. Both false and real guilt tend to be about what we do while shame makes us believe we are less of a person for it.

For example, if Jennifer gets a poor grade in a class because she didn't work hard enough, she will likely experience some guilt as a result, knowing that she could have and should have exerted more effort in her preparation.

However, if her father, after seeing her grade, tells her that she will never amount to anything, Jennifer will not only undergo a surge of guilt, but will also feel flooded with a sense of shame. She has in her mind been labeled as *broken* and discarded, a throwaway, a useless human being.

Guilt tends to slow us down at times, but *shame stops us* in our tracks! Even the phrase in English, *Shame on you*, makes most of us cringe and want to run away.

Many people experience shame every time they do something noteworthy, unable to accept praise and applause from others. They retreat from accolades to the more familiar ground of self-degradation and introspection.

Shame causes people to anesthetize their hurt even more. Some do it abusively using drugs, alcohol, illicit sex, family violence, and the like. Others dull the hurt more acceptably by working more, adding greater responsibility at church, getting better grades, being nicer.

If we are to experience and enjoy a fruitful, stimulating, forward-moving walk with God, then we will need to lay our shame down at the trailhead and give it to Jesus to carry. He died and rose again so that we don't have to ever again feel ashamed in spite of what anyone else says or will say about us.

We can reclaim our personhood, even through tears of sadness and grief over unresolved relationships, and begin to take first tentative steps of freedom toward hope and peace.

A sense of helplessness.

I counseled with a young woman named Maria, who said she was struggling with her relationship with her husband Peter. However, Maria had an interesting way of coping with her frustrations. She would go into her room, close all the drapes, turn on the television and then get into bed, pull the covers up to her chin and stay there for hours each day.

Maria felt powerless, as though there was nothing she could do to change her life or the future of her family. She saw a huge mountain in her way over which she could never climb, and thus retreated to a fantasy world where at least something was in her control!

She had never been told about her freedom to choose, a freedom that she still owned in spite of her difficult circumstances. If only Maria could have latched on to Paul's wonderfully honest, personal and powerful declaration in II Corinthians 4:8ff:

"We are afflicted in every way, but not crushed; perplexed, but not despairing; persecuted, but not forsaken; struck down, but not

destroyed; always carrying about in the body the dying of Jesus, that the life of Jesus also may be manifested in our body."

Once-changed-always-changed thinking

Whenever I see a book, seminar, message or article that starts with, *Ten Ways to...*, *The Four Secrets,* or something comparable, I get nervous. Although I know it's not always intended as such, the impression from titles like these is that there is a clear set of steps to conquer your problem or concerns! And when you completer thos you will have arrived!

I suppose that if a person is making a cake, then following certain steps will help the average baker to make a pretty decent dessert! However, when it comes to life, five or ten or even a hundred well-ordered steps may not accomplish the desired change. And even if they do, the change isn't guaranteed to last.

If we're moving into a new ministry, there's no assurance that we'll always have terrific results or enjoyable people to work with. If we're trying to express our feelings to our spouse, he or she may not respond favorably. *Change is messy.*

Maybe that's why the apostle John was careful to remind us about the progressive nature of our growth. *Someday* we will be like Him, he said, as I noted earlier. Paul echoed a similar truth in Romans 8:29, explaining that we have been, *"predestined to be conformed to the image of His son,"* the However, the process is still ongoing.

In fact, most of the Christian life is to be lived in an *ing* mode. It's ever changing, moving towards a goal, evolving. For example, Romans 8:13, 14 says: *"If by the Spirit you are putting to death the deeds of the body, you will live. For all who are being led by the Spirit of God, these are the son of God."*

We can never say we have arrived! The story goes that there was a famous mountain in the Alps climbed by hundreds of able-bodied climbers each year. It was a long climb and rather difficult but the view from the top was stupendous.

Because of the mountain's popularity, however, the local officials decided that perhaps a small chalet should be expanded part way up, giving the adventurers a more luxurious resting place along the way.

And so, they remodeled and expanded the structure and it was quite impressive to say the least. A roaring fire and the smell of hot chocolate greeted each hiker as they entered from the cool mountain air. A huge picture window framed a most magnificent mountain vista that could easily be stared at for hours.

Interestingly, after several months in operation, the chalet owners noticed that more and more hikers were remaining at the chalet for extended periods of time and fewer and fewer climbers went on to the summit. Somehow the comforts of half way were beginning to lull people into the complacency of settling for second best.

The same can happen to us as Christ followers. Halfway can start to become comfortable. Commit now to go all the way to the top in your walk with Christ!

Some Things To Take Along

Repentance.

Repent isn't really a common word these days, is it? Sometimes it can still be found on the side of a cliff along a steep mountain road accompanied by, *"Prepare to meet thy God!"* In that context, it sounds like something only a weird fanatic would say to disinterested people who drive by.

However, if we're going to venture into NOW living and put aside our excuses, we'll need to turn away from the sin or selfishness that added to the problem. Repent literally means to *"change one's mind or purpose."*

Others have described it as a turning around and going the other direction. The bottom line is that we must face our own wrong thinking that has kept us stuck, trapped and content to stay put.

But you may rightfully ask, "*Wait a minute! Since when must I repent of sin when it was my father's abusiveness that made me cautious and fearful of being close to my spouse? I'm not the sinner, he is!*"

And of course, you are right in one sense. Your father is the guilty party when it comes to your abuse. You don't need to repent of your father's sin. He must do that! Neither should any of us repent of parenting sins of rejection, bosses who mistreated us or ministry partners who misused us.

Instead, we must face the sin of seeking our own comfort from the pain and other outcomes our way. When we could have gone to God, the God of all comfort, II Corinthians 1:3, we chose our own painkillers like work, ministry, depression, humor, niceness, etc...

Unfortunately, many Christian counselors and coaches succeed only in helping their clients to change their anesthetic. Thus, people who used to dull their emotional aches with alcohol now soothe them with fulfilling ministry. Compulsive shoppers might substitute compulsive evangelism. The results are not people heading in new directions, just parallel ones, ones which look more acceptable to the naked eye of those watching.

Truly repentant people, however, will make the hard decision to venture in a different direction, in many cases towards what they fear the most! Now they begin to move forward, perhaps nervously, but obedient nonetheless, believing that God IS enough to sustain them no matter how difficult, painful or challenging circumstances prove to be.

For example, the wife who has been yearning for years to tell her husband that she is hurting, but out of fear of not being a good wife has kept silent, must repent of her self-protection and see her actions as sinful. Her new direction must be towards her husband, moving slowly, yet honestly, towards him, expressing her feelings of inadequacy, discouragement and loneliness.

Her husband may reject her feelings, not listen or become terribly defensive, none of which will cause her to feel warm and good all over. Nevertheless, she is now living godly and obediently, ultimately moving in a new direction. She is also expressing the good that God placed within her when she became His child in the first place.

God's rope of love and acceptance.

Obviously, God does not tie literal ropes around us. However, his unconditional love is enough to sustain us from any fall we believe might be fatal. Remember my adventure on the *Burma Bridge*? I didn't experience the power of the safety rope behind me that I couldn't see until I began to lean and walk. I was wobbly and scared in the process but that's what reminded me that I was still okay.

Our Christian pilgrimage will require that we test the power of God's love for us by venturing onto paths of obedience and faithfulness that we would have never traveled before.

For example, maybe you have been striving for much of your life to gain your father's acceptance, to just once have dad say, *"I'm proud of you."* During your teens and early twenties, you tried everything to get him to notice you such as good grades in school, getting the right jobs, raising good kids and yet nothing has worked.

Now you have pretty much given up. You rarely share your accomplishments with dad. *"What would it matter?"* you think. *"He wouldn't care anyway."* In fact, you have drawn away emotionally from your dad further and further, to the point where you don't care to be with him. Ironically, you also rarely attempt anything new with others, such as teaching at church or running the block party in your neighborhood.

Will God's rope hold? How will you find out? It's doing the right thing, something different, making mistakes and taking risks but realizing you didn't die.

If God does love us unconditionally and if He does see worth in us no matter our present state, then we ought to be able to mess up and not have our personhood disappear in the process, right? There's only one way to find out. Venture out to where you might fall – take a risk.

The bungee cord craze that surged years ago now still provides what may be one of the best visual examples of what I mean. People get up on top of a high bridge or crane, have a bungee cord attached to their ankles, and jump off, accelerating at breakneck speed towards the ground or water below.

Since the cord won't stretch farther than the distance to the surface below, they are soon caught by the rope (hopefully?) and bounce up and down for a while until they reach a state of equilibrium.

These brave (or stupid, depending on your point of view) souls make their jumps by believing wholeheartedly in one very important concept that, *the rope will hold!* If it doesn't, they're dead.

In the same way, we'll have to risk death by embracing the plans and steps God requires of us, learning firsthand that the rope really won't break! We'll experience the *exhilarating terror* I spoke of in chapter four. (More on this in the last chapter).

Risk-taking may additionally mean sharing a recent accomplishment, big or small, with your uncomplimentary father, clinging to the truth that no matter what his reaction is, God's rope around your personhood will hold securely.

You are still important, you still matter, and you are still lovable, even if your dad never responds! You can be deeply sad when he doesn't notice your skills, but at liberty to move on and be all that God intended you to be in spite of his response.

You won't keep accounts of your dad's insensitivity, but act in loving ways towards him nonetheless. You won't need to pretend that everything is alright or manipulate him to notice you.

The Bible often refers to our freedom in Christ, and yet it is so rare when we enjoy the enormity of it. But as we gain a sense of what it means to be permanently held by God's rope of love and acceptance, genuine change and ministry can begin to occur.

Husbands can come to their wives discouraged and overwhelmed, set free from having to have it all together all the time. Employees can approach their bosses NOT knowing everything, free to make mistakes or to come up short.

As you recall I have always struggled with not being very mechanical. (Remember my cousin Terry story?)

As I began to understand (and it took a long time) that my worth was not tied up in my ability to be handy, and that God only asked me to be responsible to care of my wife as best as I could, I was freed to venture to the homes and workshops of my mechanical friends, Keith or Jeff or Phil and ask for help.

Was there a risk? You bet there was. It was very possible that they would laugh at me (or at least to themselves) and wonder what kind of a man would need help for something so simple.

Or would they say as they saw me coming, *"Oh boy, here comes Mr. Klutz again! I wonder what he wants this time?"* After years of pretending that I was mechanically competent and accruing a score of horror stories about my flubs in the garage, I was finally able to risk being unacceptable to others, knowing that in God's sight I was still OK as a man, father, and husband.

I was now liberated to meet my family's mechanical needs right then and there, even if it required someone else's assistance. I didn't need to wait for *someday* anymore, the time when I thought I would turn into the *Tool Man*, a *someday* which likely would never come.

People in full-time ministry can also find freedom when a program or relationship doesn't go as they had hoped. They don't have to work a little bit harder, talk to just one more person, or attend just one more meeting to be acceptable in their ministry. Their efforts can be wisely chosen and less driven by unmet needs or a craving to matter.

It is no surprise to me that much of my regular counseling load while in a private counseling agency involved interacting with people in full-time Christian ministry. I see this same struggle for competence again now in those I have worked with outside the church.

I hear their cries of, *"I must perform well, I simply cannot let anybody down."* However, if we can't fail within the ministry God has led us to, we need to change our thinking about ministry or get out!

It's vital that we learn to give our best in our leadership without demanding that everyone be pleased with us all the time. In fact, too many churches and other organizations are led by people using their position to solidify their worth.

Nourishment

Remember the Christian walk is more a marathon than a sprint. You'll need sustenance on a regular basis. Where does it come from?

First and foremost from the Bible. We must be feeding on the scriptures if we are to have the strength it will take to move forward. But a mere habitual, casual or obligatory reading will not do. Feeding means carefully selecting passages that are edible, sections that your spiritual body is able to digest.

To be fed as humans our food must get to the parts of our bodies where it can do some good. Spiritually, we must allow the pages of the Bible to penetrate our minds, wills and actions so we can't help but be changed in some way. We must renew our minds with truth, not error. (Romans 12: 2) Only God's Word is consistent enough to do that every time.

Southern Gospel group, the *Gaither Vocal Band* sang a song a while back containing a great question, *"I hear you're into the Word, but is the Word getting into you?"* We will need to concentrate on the never-changing truths of scripture if they are going to get into us (Luke 2:19), even touching scars left over from previous injuries.

Meditation has become somewhat of a historical relic for many Christians, but it should have been revived long ago. Try taking just the phrase from *Psalm 56:9, "This I know, that God is for me,"* and think about it for several minutes at least. How different you and I would be if we began to grasp the significance of that one amazing truth!

We can also be nourished through *prayer*. So often our prayers are attempts to impress God, when what He desires most is our honest, child-like interactions, even though they may be at times filled with fear, discouragement and frustration.

God longs to touch us and reenergize us as only a loving Father would do. Although we may feel as though we have been crucified, God is big enough to resurrect us!

If we understand the Christian life as a walk, then concepts like, *"Pray without ceasing"* (I Thessalonians 5:17) make more sense. We will be in regular prayer, realizing that Jesus walks with us in everything we do. He is always present. When Solomon writes, *"In all your ways acknowledge Him,"* (Proverbs 3:6) he indicates that he, too, understands that God is ever-present.

Prayer must also include listening to hear what God is saying to us that very moment. Jesus promised that He would be with us always!

Try something today.

Before you begin your next activity, simply acknowledge that God is there. Picture Jesus Himself if that is easier. Either way stop and recognize the presence of God. What attitude will you take into that activity? Are you afraid? Go together with the Lord. Will this be a major jump? He will go with you and hold your hand until His rope of love grabs you.

Your praying can become a fresh, rich conversation with God instead of a dreaded routine. You won't just know about God, but you will begin to know Him intimately.

You will also need the nourishment of *others*. God is big enough to meet our every need by Himself and yet He has chosen to use others to help us stay on the right path and to keep going

The New Testament is full of "one another" phrases like, build up one another, encourage one another, strengthen one another.

We must allow others into our lives who will keep us truthful about how to live life God's way. They can help us to keep moving towards our fears, not running away, practicing overcoming past sinful habits and thinking God's thoughts.

Our tendency, unfortunately, is to accumulate friendships who merely strengthen our sinfulness, who coddle us and buy into our pity, blaming and self-protection. These individuals encourage us to stay in *someday* living rather than risk the excitement and fulfillment of moving forward NOW.

If you can, join a small group or Bible study that promotes loving openness, accountable progress and biblical thinking. Make sure they are people who can remind you of who you are in Christ.

Find a close friend, a NOW person, who will have the candor and commitment to you to be lovingly honest.

(Ephesians 4: 15) Sometimes your best friend isn't the best person because they like you too much to be honest.

Time

We need time to stop and enjoy your progress along the way. We are so caught up these days in final products that we miss the enjoyment of the process to get there. Sex has become like that, hasn't it? Married couples often concentrate on the sexual summit of orgasm, forgetting the wonderful enjoyment that can be experienced getting there.

Similarly, many Christians (and churches for that matter) continue to remind themselves that they are not perfect yet, so they strive onward, somehow energized one more time by the knowledge that someday they'll be at the peak of their Christian life.

But remember, our peak will not ultimately come until we meet the Lord in the air. (I Thessalonians 4: 16). Everything up to that point is below the summit. Stop and enjoy the sights along the way.

As my kids, wife and I have made our climbs, we would stop now and then and look at the mountain springs, the beautiful vistas, the piles of snow in July and the marmots scurrying across the rocks. The summit was our goal, but amazingly the journey also became part of our experience.

Sadly, many believers believe it unspiritual to relax now and then, to delight in the headway they have made up until now. Yes, the apostle Paul did challenge us to *"Press on toward the goal,"* (Philippians 3:14) but he also reminded his friends at Philippi that they were free to live joyfully in the present: *"The things you have learned and received and heard and seen in me, practice these things; and the God of peace shall be with you."* (4:9)

Remember that time, *the tyranny of the urgent* as one author coined it, is one of the great enemies of NOW living. Always being pulled by the call to perfection will sap your energy as you take new steps forward. Your perfect world will always be just a little bit farther from you than it is right now.

The good news is that you can slow down, do less worrying and still be a person of value, worth and success.

So Where Do You Start?

Take inventory.

Lay your *somedays* before God and a few caring friends. What have you been putting off that God has nudged you to start now? What has kept you from it? The *someday* of securities, responsibilities, or relationships? What fuels have you been constantly burning to sustain your *someday* thinking? Fear? Fantasies? Frenzy?

Go back to the questions at the end of each chapter and summarize where you are. On the surface, looking at your current state and patterns of living will not necessarily be an enjoyable experience. However, remember you are bringing yourself, sin and all, before God Himself, who still loves you in spite of it all.

Prioritize.

What do you need to work on first? What will your first steps be? Which errant paths did you identify in the last chapter? The launching pads that are most terrifying to you may be those that need the most attention. What are the hindrances that hold you back? You cannot change everything at once. If you try, you will simply walk face to face into a mountain you could never climb.

You'll feel like you're trying to ascend *Mt. Everest* when you're only prepared for the *Smokies*. Ask God to bring to the surface those areas that are most essential to your getting unstuck from the quicksand of *someday*. *You can't do everything but you can do something!*

Pray for a change in direction

Ask God to forgive you for caring for your own worth, trying to find life and fulfillment apart from Him. Admit that you've sought love from people and in places that could never ultimately complete you. Tell Him how you have demanded that life and its circumstances turn out a certain way before you would be totally obedient to His will. Express that you're sorry for letting the actions, decisions and feelings of others dictate how you live.

Let Him know that you will not make grandiose promises any more, but instead begin to walk one step at a time, acknowledging that He is present in all that you do, that He is your only source of ultimate worth, love and value. In other words, repent! Is that word making more sense?

When our kids were little, my mother-in-law made a very wise statement about childrearing that I have never forgotten. *"You may not always know what your kids will do,"* she said, *"but your kids need to always know what you'll do!"* Obviously, her point was that we needed to know ahead of time what our rules and guidelines were and then be sure that our kids knew we would stick to them.

In a similar way, we need to do the same as we think about moving forward in our Christian lives. We don't know what will happen tomorrow, much less five years from now, so we must decide now what we will live and die for, no matter what.

The story is told of Sir Oliver Wendell Homes, former Supreme Court justice and statesman, who was riding on a train during his later years of life. When the conductor came down the aisle to punch his ticket, however, Judge Holmes began going through his pockets looking for his ticket.

The young conductor, who had seen Holmes many times on the train, smiled and said graciously, *"Mr.*

Holmes, it is quite okay if you can't find your ticket. I know you are an honest man."

Mr. Holmes nonetheless responded with a quizzical look and said, *"My young man, the problem is not that I cannot find my ticket. The problem is that I don't know where I am going!"* God knows the way for you.

Find out what it is. You'll never hit your target without having one that you can clearly see.

Get rid of unnecessary encumbrances -

Are you bitter? Ask God to start removing the strands of bitterness in you. Forgive someone who needs forgiveness. If need be, write that letter that you will never send to a parent for example, spewing out the anger and resentment you've had over the years. Then tear the letter up. Face your pain and cut the strings from the hurt that has limited you for so long.

Commit yourself to a life that no longer blames others for your condition, even though they may have played a resounding role in your past. Seek God out to help you live as a new creature, hurting at times, yes, but liberated to walk onward step by step. *"As you have therefore received Christ Jesus the Lord, so walk in Him." (Colossians 2:6)*

If time is a hindering factor to your progress, determine selected activities that you will eliminate from your weekly schedule to allow you to pursue godly and obedient goals.

Plan a small "jump."

Remember the bungee cord illustration? At some point in time must test whether the rope will hold, and begin our walk down one of the paths we know God is asking of us. Look at one of the areas He is challenging you to work on or the ministry plans He is speaking to you about. Contemplate how you could take a small first step, one to get you started on your walk.

From high wire performers to the Acapulco cliff-divers, all of them begin with simple accomplishments before they get to a finished product. We can do the same. If you have had trouble communicating with your children out of fear that you wouldn't know what to say, try beginning with simply, *"Tell me about your day at school."*

The issue is not whether your conversation lasts two hours after that, but whether YOU approached your child with love, interest and concern!

If you've been putting off seminary training, you could begin by simply writing for some information and finding out more. You are moving now; you have taken a step and YOU DID NOT DIE!

You may need to speak to a parent about a difficult issue in their treatment of your children. Your first steps may include setting up a time to talk in the near future. But *someday* is no longer controlling you, you are controlling *someday*. If something needs to wait or be placed on hold, you decide. The next chapter will deal with that in more detail.

Regularly evaluate your progress.

One of the best ways to monitor your walk is to meet with others on a consistent basis. Let your Bible study, small group, prayer partner, counselor, mentor, pastor or whoever know what your goals are, what typically gets in your way and what you'll try in the next week or two. Make sure that your friends are willing to be candid with you and not simply tell you what you want to hear.

A journal, in which you can record your thoughts, fears, frustrations and accomplishments plus have a record of your progress to look back on, is also helpful. Make specific entries in it, detailing your joys and disappointments, victories along with your defeats.

So, start your walk slowly and enjoy the scenery along the way and someday you can hopefully hear God say, *"Well done, good and faithful servant!"*

Gary Sinclair

Things To Think About In Chapter 8

What might you be tempted to bring to your NOW living journey that could just get in the way or weigh you down?

What could be a good first or next step for you that you've been putting off to take?

What things came to mind from this chapter to bring along on your journey that you know will help you keep going?

WATCHING YOUR WAIT`
CHAPTER 9

"He that can have patience can have what he will."
Benjamin Franklin

We Americans spend hours and hours waiting, don't we? Drive-thru's, banks, ticket centers, elevators, doctors' offices, online chats, company help lines, traffic jams and more can put us on hold for hours each week. Most people use their smart phone to break up the down time but that can get old, too.

One of the most enjoyable boredom–busters I've ever encountered was the use of a mime to entertain the visitors before one of the special acts at Sea World. Since this particular show was very popular, people would begin to enter the auditorium twenty minutes or more before the program began, hoping to find good seats.

Around fifteen minutes before show time, a mime came out into the audience and helped direct people to their seats in an incredibly humorous and creative way. He would sneak behind people and imitate their walk, make hilarious faces at babies and stick out his tongue at those he sensed didn't appreciate his help! The excited audience had a hilarious time laughing, making the pre-show wait seem much shorter.

In spite of technology's continual improvements, waiting is still a fact of life and we must accept delays in far more important situations. Solomon understood this when he wrote in Ecclesiastes 3, *"There is an appointed time for everything. And there is a time for every event under Heaven.* The Psalms often suggest that waiting is a regular part of God's plan and responses.

So, how does waiting fit into our battle against the *Someday Syndrome?* How do we know when to wait and when to push on NOW as we've discussed for much of the book so far?

A Biblical Perspective

In the Bible, signs and wonders were often used to help with decisions. One of the earliest and most unusual methods included employing what was known as the *urim and thummim.* Although no one seems to have the final explanation of this strategy, many scholars believe these strange objects to have been gems or precious stones, placed into the breastplate of the high priest.

They used three to as many as twelve gems, the latter number representing the tribes of Israel. Either way these odd paragons were employed at times to determine God's specific will or plan for the people.

But there were other methods as well. Moses heard from God through a burning bush, the children of Israel followed a cloud and fire, while the wise men seeking baby Jesus relied on a star to guide them.

Most of these methods have vanished from God's current ways of doing things. Nonetheless, many of us still long to receive clearer signs about what to do next. Usually we simply want to know the right and best way, God's way, the wisest route to take on life's journeys.

Wouldn't people without jobs, parents agonizing over their rebellious teen's future and singles wondering if they will ever marry love to have a specific plan for success?

Instead we have been given the Bible as the starting point and foundation from which through the Holy Spirit decipher the attitudes, directions, thoughts and behaviors God wants us to incorporate into everyday life.

That's it. We generally don't get special gems, prophets with final answers or burning bushes. However, it is important for those of us caught in the *Someday Syndrome* to ponder the balance between living in the now and waiting on God for better outcomes.

Psalm 27: 14 says, *"Wait for the Lord; be strong and take heart and wait for the Lord." "I wait for the LORD, my soul waits, and in his Word I put my hope. (Psalm 130:5)* The prophet Isaiah reminds us, *"Those who hope in the LORD will renew their strength. (40:31)*

The last thing Christianity needs is a group of inconsiderate, bull-in-the-china-shop individuals who run through life demanding that God give them an exact answer every time they ask.

Remember a typical *Someday Syndromer* primarily waits to act to be protected from rejection, failing or somehow looking bad. Choosing to wait until tomorrow is almost always prompted by nervous fear rather than joyful anticipation.

A NOW-guided person chooses to wait because of scriptural directives and wisdom from God. Waiting for them neither serves as a safety valve from personal injury nor as a dreaded consequence of following God's direction

It is interesting that in the Old Testament there are several different words used to translate our word *wait*. The first word *qavah* is used most often and means to *wait with anticipation or eagerness*. In the Psalms alone, qavah is utilized on thirteen different occasions. It is typically contained in verses encouraging us to wait on God in the middle of difficulty.

For example, Psalm 37: 9: *"For evildoers will be cut off, But those who wait for the Lord, they will inherit the land."* The same word is used again in that chapter, verse thirty-four: *"Wait for the Lord, and keep His way, And He will exalt you to inherit the land; When the wicked are cut off, you will see it."*

Delays are chosen or accepted as loving acts of our caring and gentle Father, the One who knows what is best for us. Appropriate *somedays* will become our allies not excuses to avoid our fears. We can trust in God Himself, not in our own machinations to protect ourselves.

A NOW person no longer demands certain outcomes in life, such as having an always loving spouse, perfectly obedient children or a job that provides sufficient praise. Instead they trust God for their worth and happiness, even when life is not going their way.

A second word for waiting is found in the Old Testament. This word, transliterated *chil,* means to "whirl around, dance or writhe." It is also translated, *to be in anguish* such as a mother giving birth.

Psalm 37:7, *"Rest in the Lord and wait patiently for Him; Do not fret because of him who prospers in his way, because of the man who carries out wicked schemes."*

It was spoken by Elihu, one of Job's friends as he scolded Job for his cries to God during an especially low moment: *"Surely God will not listen to an empty cry, Nor will the Almighty regard it. How much less when you say you do not behold Him, and you must wait for Him!"*

Waiting can be painful. Anguish and despair often precede hope. Pain is never enjoyable, but the context makes a difference. My wife Jackie has spoken of the pain-filled hours she endured while waiting for our son Tim and daughter Amy to be born. But I have never heard her refer to those times as tragic, unfulfilling or needless.

She now looks back on the hurt as the forerunner to the blessing of bearing a child. Her pain came while waiting for the joy to follow.

I wrote another song after Amy was born (equal time, right?) that highlights this truth:

Amy's Song

It was a beautiful sun-filled morning
When I saw this new child of mine,
As she started to cry, then so did I,
Overcome by joy Divine,
In the fulness of time, God made her mine,
Oh, these moments are so very few,
Thank you, Lord, for this one,
Who in love now has come from You.

Chorus
Thank you, Lord, for that moment,
For the chance to see life begin,
To see how great a God you are,
To know how life's changed since you've come in,
Thank you, Lord, for that moment
When this new life came into view,
Oh, it's nothing I did
And there's no one to praise but You.

There was also a day many years ago,
When new life came in to Me,
I'd heard that Jesus died and was crucified,
And now He lives to set me free,
So, I asked Him in to forgive my sin,
And I was born anew that day,
And today I know that He'll love me so always.

G. Sinclair, 1983

Someday Syndromers rarely look forward to joy, blessing, and fulfillment. Instead, they spend a lot of time and energy avoiding risks, potential injury or hurt because of fear. For them, waiting is an excuse, barrier, or protection from changing or serving others. They believe it's their insurance against failure, rejection and not getting love.

But NOW Christians wait, accepting that God has a purpose and plan which may also require delays. Isaiah 40: 31 reminds us, *"Yet those who wait for the Lord will gain new strength. They will mount up with wings like eagles, They will run and not get tired, they will walk and not become weary."*

Some Important Waits

I am always surprised when someone wants to do something that is a clear violation of scripture. And yet many believe that their being faithful and obedient the rest of the time will balance out the misdeed.

I think of Arlene who made tremendous progress as she went through a messy divorce. She had suffered damaging verbal and physical abuse and yet grew spiritually, attended Bible studies, and regularly attended church again. In fact, she began to understand her worth in Christ in spite of her difficult past.

However, it wasn't long before Arlene approached me about living with another man, one who was also recently divorced, a neophyte Christian and struggling emotionally. When I suggested her choices were unwise, Arlene responded as though I had overlooked all the other progress she had made.

But in reality, Arlene was longing for the closeness of a relationship again, one in which she was cared for and special. She was finding it difficult to wait for circumstances that God directed His way and in accordance with Scripture.

What might God be asking you to put off when he says, *Wait?*

Perfection

Flawlessness is one of those fantasies we live for much of the time. We want the perfect church, job, spouse, family, world. As a result, we live the lie that everything in our world is okay, that nothing is wrong, that God is blessing and that we couldn't be happier.

Everyone thinks we are on top of our world. In fact, if someone were to ask us, we would agree that our life is pretty great. At this point we don't see the flaws in us because we're okay, at least from our perspective.

And yet all is not well. Some of the most perfectionistic people I know are those who have some segment of their lives recklessly out of control, whether they know it or not! Many have histories of abuse and never want to risk being hurt again, so they keep their relationships manicured and proper.

Others are wondering about their ability to provide for their families, so they voraciously work at controlling potential crashes in other parts of their worlds, such as church or home. Jane from an earlier chapter was like this. Her insides were churning with guilt over past indiscretions while her present relationships were a shambles and she had just lost her job.

And yet to look at her, she was a picture of perfection from her clothes to her notetaking during our sessions. She didn't want to miss a thing! But many times, when tears would well up in her eyes while she reflected on her past hurts, I would see her shut them off just as quickly, not wanting to appear broken or out of control.

Nonetheless, perfection must wait until we get to Heaven. It's okay for us to be less than God wants us to be. Romans 8:29 reminds us that we are to be *conformed to the image of His Son.* We are on our way, but we are not there yet. Someday, though, *we shall be like Him.* (1 John 3: 2) That's Good News!

Total fulfillment.

Andy found himself walking alone towards a beautiful and yet radiant light. Though by himself, he sensed someone else was there, too, an unknown, but inviting force beckoning him onward. He remembered that only moments ago he was driving down a busy highway in his home town of Waterville, on his way home from the store where he had picked up a few groceries for mom.

"*This is heaven*," he thought excitedly to himself, and he found himself pulled almost magnetically toward the light which had attracted him upon his arrival. Just a few steps further he began to see the hazy shape of someone, and he now knew all along that the One ahead had been drawing him all along.

Within moments Andy heard the most soothing and caring voice he had ever encountered and it spoke to him gently, "*Welcome home, Andy. I have been waiting for you.*"

A person in magnificent light, who Andy now knew to be Jesus Himself, reached out His nail-scarred hand and pulled Andy to his chest. All was well. Every care, longing, and struggle had vanished.

This is obviously a fictional account of a young man's death and subsequent journey to Heaven, but it vividly reminds us that we will never know completeness and total satisfaction until we meet the Savior face to face.

I John 3:2 reminds us of that truth so clearly, *"Beloved, now we are children of God, and it has not as yet appeared what we shall be, but we know that when He appears we shall be like Him because we shall see Him just as He is."*

It is essential that we comprehend that nothing in this world - relationships, tasks, accomplishments, activities – is capable of totally satisfying us. At best those things can gratify temporarily. But our longing for more will surface repeatedly whether we like it or not. While at first glance, this state of things may seem depressing, it is freeing once we understand and accept it.

For example, when I realize that my children cannot ever totally satisfy me, as hard as they may try or as desperately as I might squeeze it out of them, I become free to love them as they are, faults and all, and train them up in the way they should go

I won't require that they come through for me, in school, sports, behaviorally, or emotionally, so that I will somehow feel whole again. I will find myself more likely to love them like Mr. Rogers always did, "*Just the way you are.*"

No circumstance or event will require our demanding that life somehow give us what we have waited for so long. We will no longer need to command bigger churches, have more loving spouses, enjoy more successful businesses, raise better children, or field winning sports teams to make us happy.

This was likely Paul's thought as he wrote to the Romans, *"Even we ourselves groan within ourselves, waiting eagerly for our adoption as sons, the redemption of our body.* (8: 23)

Spiritual maturity.

Every now and then I get the urge to play the guitar. I'm in one of those stages now even as I write. As a pianist, songwriter, bassist and vocalist, I have a pretty strong musical background. I often sit down though and pick up this more foreign instrument, the guitar, in my hands.

But I'm disappointed. My fingers which move so agilely on the keyboard seem arthritic on the neck of the guitar. Instead of relishing the freedom to make music that I typically enjoy, I stumble from one chord to another, desperately wishing that something more melodious would flow from my feeble attempts. Soon I quit in frustration, returning to my comfortable place at the piano or bass.

What I want is instant success. I know how glorious the guitar can sound. I have several good friends who are true artists. But in typical baby-boomer fashion I demand to sound like they do NOW !

Unfortunately, many believers get caught in the same trap, wanting their spiritual growth to occur quickly, overnight, unwilling to offer God the hard work of discipline, practice and waiting that spiritual growth requires. Maturing is especially challenging for a person who becomes a Christian later in life.

She joins the family of God, often not realizing that she enters this new relationship as a spiritual baby and thus must begin life so to speak with rudimentary ideas and simple food.

And yet Peter's challenge must be embraced no matter what our chronological age is, *"Like newborn babies, crave pure spiritual milk, so that by it you may grow up in your salvation, now that you have tasted that the Lord is good. (I Peter 2:2)*

And as the writer of Hebrews says, *"Solid food is for the mature, who by constant use have trained themselves to distinguish good from evil."* I Peter 2: 2. There are no shortcuts to growth in God's family. We will have to wait and let good nutrition bear fruit and in us in due time!

God's timing.

He was a model man of God. He obeyed his father in the middle of imminent dangers. He had graciously suffered the mistreatment of his family in spite of a grim future ahead of him. He resisted the day to day sexual advances of his boss' wife, standing firm that he would not sin against the God he loved.

Placed into prison, he quickly advanced to leadership over the prisoners, yet his heart naturally ached to one day be free. When two of his fellow prisoners requested interpretation of their dreams, he willingly obliged asking only one simple request of them in return. *"Only keep me in mind when it goes well with you, and please do me a kindness by mentioning me to Pharaoh, and get me out of this house."*

Joseph, son of Jacob, longed to be liberated from the prison sentence he never really deserved. His ordeal had been far too long already, at least in human terms, and his mistreatment was cruel at best.

And yet, it took two full years before Joseph finally experienced true freedom, before he was actually vindicated, an incredible 13 years from the beginning of his ordeal.

God obviously had bigger plans for Joseph, future happenings which required a heavenly timetable.

As we continue to climb on our journey with Christ, there will come moments, months, even years, when we will have conceivably done everything right, in total obedience to God, with as pure motives as are humanly possible, and we will still have to wait for God to respond to us.

Or instead, He will act in ways that seem totally out of line with what we perceive to be rational thinking. The baby we had put off having until next year comes now. We cannot find work and our money has run out. A loved one dies unexpectedly. Our church doesn't grow to the size we had envisioned and programs and staff must be cut .

Our personal mentor moves out of the area and we are left alone. These events were likely a result of timing, not someone's failures or mistakes. We can't blame anyone. God simply allowed or caused these things to happen and we must wait to know their purpose, in this life or the next.

With Job we may lament, *"For what I fear comes upon me, and what I dread befalls me. am not at ease, nor am I quiet, And I am not at rest, but turmoil comes." (3: 25, 26)*

And yet, we can live free to trust God in all his sovereignty and magnificence and remain satisfied to wait for him to do His work in His time. We may become anxious but we don't have to panic, we may become saddened but not despairing, we may become angry but without vengeance.

With David we can say, *"I waited patiently for the Lord, and He inclined to me and heard my cry. He brought me up out of the pit of destruction, out of the miry clay; and He set my feet upon a rock making my footsteps firm. (Psalm 40:1,2)*

The big picture.

A few years ago, my family had just opened a new game (at the time) called *Outburst*. You may have played it. Oddly, we decided to read the directions first just to make sure we knew what we were doing.

But as we began to scan the rules we were greeted by this rather unusual statement in bold letters: "WARNING: THIS GAME IS NOT FAIR." The reason it wasn't fair was that the categories such as, "things under the sink," "movies that have one-word titles," and "ingredients in a cake" were selected by the game's designers ahead of time.

As we began to play, we realized the words on the box were correct. It wasn't fair!

At times, life really is like OUTBURST. From a human perspective, it is frightfully unfair. Loved ones die before their time. Jackie's brother passed away at sixty from the same cancer Jackie had. Some experience good health, we endure chronic pain.

Friends are physically beautiful. We are homely. In some nations Christians live in abundance, others barely survive. Certain babies are born healthy, others begin life with enormous handicaps.

Unfortunately, many well-meaning people would say that those who struggle do so because of some sin in person's life or family. And while sinful acts can lead to big problems that cannot be blamed on others or God, many cannot be explained in those terms.

And if those who make the *caused by sin claim* were honest they would realize that they cannot live by this view of life themselves. Sometimes things just happen. Claiming, blaming and shaming at that point do not provide relief or answers.

The thousands who lost their lives in the World Trade Center and Pentagon bombings or the students shot at Columbine or those who died in Oklahoma City were certainly not treated fairly! More recent tragedies, some not as well-known, but just as tragic, aren't fair either.

Back in the 80's three godly men were flying back to the Detroit area in a private plane from a speaking ministry engagement. The pilot was extremely experienced and the other two brothers were known for their passionate commitments to Christ.

The three friends and their families were also known for their theology which promoted thinking that Christians never needed to be sick and would be protected if they would just trust God and claim the result they wanted.

It was a most unusual winter morning in February when they were to return. Snow lingered on the ground, but the temperature was unseasonably warm and a dense fog blanketed the city and its surrounding suburbs.

However, instead of the fog burning off as the temperature warmed, the clouds never budged. The two brothers, in the hands of their experienced pilot, attempted a landing that morning, hit several power wires and crashed to the ground, their bodies badly burned.

Was it fair to leave these wives without husbands and their children without daddies? No, of course not, but it happened. Was it fair that another pilot might have made it but this one did not? No. Was it fair when Rick Husband, a committed follower of Christ, died in the Columbia disaster, along with his esteemed and talent colleagues?

We could name thousands of others since, some famous, some not, who passed way too young and there's only one human answer. It's not fair.

You see, the only consolation for much of the seeming injustice in our world today will come one day when we see the big picture and for that we must wait. Faith is not so much believing in something we know for sure as it is in believing as though *someday* we will know for sure! For now, we must rely only on what we do know, leaving the rest to Jesus for now.

Philip Yancey in his now classic book, *Disappointment with God*, puts it this way, *"By no means can we infer that our own trials are, like Job's, specially arranged by God to go settle some decisive issue in the universe. But we can safely assume that our limited range of vision will in similar fashion distort reality. Pain narrows vision. . . . The big picture, with the whole universe as a backdrop, includes much activity that we never see."*

During one of my studies of the Lord's Prayer in Matthew chapter six, I looked at each word in this magnificent text. I attempted to see its context throughout the rest of the book, especially within the Sermon on the Mount in chapters 5 - 7.

I noticed something very interesting as I considered the word, "Father," found in the phrase, "*Our Father, who art in Heaven.*" The word *"father"* is used sixteen times in the Sermon on the Mount alone! Jesus was evidently trying to emphasize God's loving role as a compassionate dad while He exhorted his followers to kingdom-like living.

Perhaps we need to be reminded that God is our Father, that He alone sees the big picture and we will one day understand it. We have all heard the story about the young adult who says, *"You know, the older I get, the smarter and smarter my dad gets."*

Someday God's disciplines will make sense, those catastrophes he allowed will fit into the tapestry we call life, and those differences we ached over will be seen as uniquenesses, not disabilities. We'll realize that suffering, heartache and disappointment were all divine tools to refine, shape and cause us to let go of our props and anesthetics that we so often use to get by.

We can beg God to tell us more now but we may only get silence in return. As C.S. Lewis described in *A Grief Observed*, "*The longer you wait, the more emphatic the silence will become.*" Larry Crabb has said more recently, "*God will never allow suffering to come into our lives that is not necessary to achieve His good purpose."*

Waiting is also used by God to force us to rest. Hockey players skate feverishly for two minutes or so but must stop and catch their breath on the bench before they are able to return to their next shift on the ice. Yes, they are waiting their turn while someone else plays but their waiting is an opportunity to get ready to serve the team again.

Proper rest gives stamina. Waiting within God's timetable builds strength.

Signs That Waiting Might Be Best

I wish that there were some nice, manageable, easy to understand formula or guide to tell us when to move or stay, go or wait, but I'm confident there isn't one that simple.

But there are a few principles and guidelines that this chapter and Scripture in general offer which can help. Start with these as you first begin to ponder your decision to wait or go ahead.

When we quit thinking so eagerly about the idea.

Yes, our own wishes and misguided passions can throw us off here, but if God's in our next step then we won't be able to shake the idea. If He's not, then our excitement will wane or other circumstances will quash the idea.

Before I started writing today, I was in the shower and began thinking about a new way to impact a group I'm working with without actually travelling there right now. I hadn't considered the idea until today. It came out of nowhere. The possibilities seem significant so I'm going to see if this is the time to move on it.

It's not wise

In spite of our desire to move now, does practical wisdom keep standing in the way? Do we keep finding logical roadblocks that make the idea way too farfetched to be practical and of God right now?

Various wise people keep telling us to wait

Proverbs suggests that with many counselors there is victory. God often uses people to share His insights and direction with us. We need to listen and if we hear more than one or two people saying the same thing then we would be smart to follow their lead.

We realize we're wanting to go for the wrong reasons

Remember what we've already discussed in significant detail. Many of our actions, decisions and demands arise out of our need to be valued, loved and significant, not God's direction. When those personal goals outweigh wisdom and God's leading we need to put the brakes on our process.

The excitement of Christmas

Waiting is never easy but it still has its rewards. The days and weeks prior to Christmas morning are usually torturous for most children, wishing so dearly that they could tear into the stack of presents marked especially for them!

My parents, however, always told my sister and me where the Christmas presents were hidden, even before they were wrapped. Mom and Dad said, *"Look, if you want to spoil the fun, excitement and surprises of Christmas morning, go ahead. If not, you will wait and not try to discover what your gifts are now."*

I only saw one gift ahead of time and that was by accident! I'm glad I waited the rest of the years. Christmas was always a wonderful day and I never had to pretend that I was ecstatic over something I already knew about.

In I Corinthians 13, the love chapter, Paul discusses the role of patience, especially when our hearts long for more. *"For now we see in a mirror dimly, but then face to face; now I know in part, but then I shall know fully just as I also have been fully known."* (v. 12)

We shouldn't wait to do those things that God tells us to do NOW and which we delay simply out of fear, discomfort or laziness. That's the focus of this book. However, there are some things worth waiting for even if everyone else demands them now.

Things To Think About in Chapter Nine

What are some recent decisions, goals and hopes that I've wisely and satisfactorily put off? Why did I(we) wait?

Are there things I'm doing that for good reason need to be stopped and delayed for now?

What was it that I feared by waiting and leaving these desires, goals and hopes in the *Someday* category

YOUNG OR OLD
CHAPTER 10

"Age is something that doesn't matter unless you are a cheese."
Luis Bunuel

I have been driving for over fifty years now but I remember the scene as though it were yesterday. After church I would sit behind the steering wheel in my parents' car imagining that I was travelling all alone down the freeway.

While the engine was quiet and I was going nowhere, my imagination raced with excitement fantasizing about whizzing around town in the family auto. But soon I would snap out of my daydream as the latch on the door popped open and mom, dad, and sister climbed into the car.

Every pretend trip made the wait seem that much longer in spite of my parents' loving encouragement, *"You'll be driving one of these days. Someday soon you'll have that license you've been wanting."*

"Why did I have to be a kid anyhow?" I still complained to myself. "How come I can't grow up sooner so I can drive?"

Getting behind the wheel of a car, of course, requires you be certain age before the state will issue that precious license. And yet much of our society has treated young people as though there is some similar age they must attain before God can use them in his kingdom-building.

Yes, our young people today act more grown up all the time, look and act like superstars and possess adult-level talents while accomplishing amazing things. They are starting Internet businesses and companies at the age when many of us used to have paper routes or begin work at some fast food place.

But to argue or dissect the social implications and impact of young people in society today goes beyond the scope of this book. Instead, as I wrap up *NOW*, I want to reemphasize how and why God throughout history has given young people significant roles in work.

We dare not allow childhood or adolescence to be another place to become stuck in the *Someday Syndrome*!

Young people must also understand their roles in God's plans and realize He can also use them NOW to make a difference, draw people to Himself and serve His church. Often, we hear well-meaning people say that young people are the future of the Church. I want to suggest that they are also part of *today's church*!

The Peter Pan Myth

Several decades ago now, Dr. Dan Kiley wrote a book called *The Peter Pan Syndrome* about men who never grow up! Interestingly, in his psychological description of a typical PPS personality, he speaks of their tendency to procrastinate, *"During the developmental stage, the young victim puts off until he is absolutely forced to do them. 'I don't know' and 'I don't care' become his defense against criticism. His life goals are fuzzy and poorly defined, mainly because he puts off thinking about them until tomorrow."*

My hunch is that teens and how adults view them hasn't changed that much since he wrote his book. We often think young people won't make much of a difference in the church, their community, office, school or wherever.

Thankfully, many young people are changing that image dramatically and we must help them keep moving forward NOW.

How do we do that? Is it even possible? Surprising at that may seem, it is. Here's how to do it, even if you're a generation or cultural norm or two apart from the nearest young person in your sphere of influence.

We must begin to think like they do!

Remember how Peter Pan and his friends flew around, mesmerized by their fantasy-controlled world, playing games and imagining all sorts of delightful, exciting and adventurous antics?

What is it that we're promoting today when the focus for many kids and their parents is always joining one more activity, learning to play one more video game and spending one more hour on their smart phone? Is it possible that we subtly cause them to feel unneeded when it comes to doing the truly important, world-changing responsibilities?

And yet for thousands of years, God enlisted young people to accomplish monumental tasks. King Joash became ruler over Judah at age seven. (II Kings 11:21) David literally rocked the world as a kid when he killed Goliath and began his ascendancy to the throne, a royal lineage that would one day bear Jesus Himself.

I particularly enjoy the story of the young boy in John, chapter six, whose bread and fish were used in the feeding of the multitudes. We know very little about him except that he apparently gave his lunch to Jesus who would multiply it enough to feed the thousands.

In recent years, we have witnessed young people taking their faith to the streets as they hold Bible studies in their schools, neighborhoods and communities, rally for prayer around the flagpole, take a stand for abstinence and give of their time and money to work in local and international missions around the world.

Unfortunately, these aren't the students who regularly receive accolades, media coverage and honors. Those who stand for what is right and noble are often the ones who are criticized most for being different while the young people who break the rules and live for themselves are called *progressives.*

Thankfully many students still stand for their faith and are often better models of vibrant, raw Christianity than us adults. Many more eagerly give their time, talents and resources to love the *least of these* in ways adults are too busy to do themselves.

Sometimes the simple naivete, boldness and innocence of the young motivates them to share their faith in real terms without the typical precautions and baggage that adults carry around.

Every Christmas program in America is another powerful lesson about the lack of inhibitions of children that can easily (and often humorously) speak volumes about the greatest story ever told, Jesus coming to earth.

I'll never forget the day when our son Tim was about 4 years old and was walking through the inner courtyard of the apartment complex where my in-laws were living. Two elderly women were sitting in their lawn chairs enjoying the warm sunshine when Tim approached.

Noticing a cute little boy coming to see them, they asked, "*Well, little guy, what is your name?* Tim proudly announced that his name was, "*Timothy Joel Sinclair.*" He also added (and I tell you this with pride) that his first and middle names were from the Bible.

One of the ladies responded, "*Oh really? I knew that Timothy was a Bible name, but I didn't know that Joel was in the Bible.*" Tim spouted back with hardly a pause for air, "*You know, lady, you really ought to read your Bible more!*" Yes, children can make a difference even if it happens in slightly embarrassing ways.

Paul was well aware of the power of youth when he wrote to young Timothy, his true child in the faith, *"Let no one look down on your youthfulness, but rather in speech, conduct, love, faith and purity, show yourself an example of those who believe. (I Timothy 4:12)*

Organizations like *Youth For Christ, Young Life, Fellowship of Christian Athletes* and *Youth With A Mission* are vivid, lasting examples of how God can mobilize young people to help reach the world for Christ. They don't have to wait for *Someday.*

So many young people continue to turn to drugs, alcohol, illicit sex, the dark web, gangs, or just hanging out with the wrong people. Why? It's likely that the majority of those kids have never been challenged with what they could do to make a difference in their community, church, school or overall culture.

In fact, current statistics suggest that millennials are leaving the church in droves.

Why? Perhaps it's because parents are often also caught in *someday thinking.* They are trapped by busyness, fear and their own fantasies so their children follow their lead and live accordingly

Expected to be sexy, worldly-wise and just as attractive as their Hollywood models and heroes, they get pressed into a surreal, faux adulthood but remain emotionally unable to manage its demands and responsibilities.

Young people need to be told they are valuable and usable for God NOW, just as they are, without any unreasonable expectations attached. They need to be given opportunities and taught to serve others, to give instead of take, to share what they have instead of getting every new product on the market as though it holds the keys to happiness.

We have perhaps overlooked the fact that studies from as far back as the 19th century have shown that the average age a person goes through a religious conversion is 15.6 years. And yet in a recent Gallup poll, while 93% of teenagers believe that God loves them, only 29% have personally experienced God's presence.

In addition, *Barna Research* shows that the most influential time period for a person to receive Christ is before age 12!

Yes, there are appropriate *somedays* for children and adolescents that should be made very clear to them. I covered some in the last chapter. Young people must learn to wait for some things, often a major challenge. Sexual relationships, full-time jobs, having children and the like are all far more enjoyable and appropriate for adults.

But helping our kids to see that NOW they still do matter to our families, churches and communities will make waiting for those other somedays much easier.

Why Youth Wait For *Someday*

They believe they're not old enough.

Some years ago, I was visiting the home of a friend named John for the very first time. John was a helper when I worked with *Youth For Christ* in New York. I had always noticed that John spoke very quickly and his voice was unusually loud. At first, I thought he spoke that way because for many years he ran the sound for a well-known rock band.

However, as I sat around his dinner table that evening, it became apparent that John's volume had little to do with his rock 'n roll background. John's mother and father were yellers and their griping, complaining and constant nagging of the children dominated the entire conversation (if you could even call it that)!

There was only one way to be heard in that house. SHOUT or speak loudly, whether someone else was talking or not! I had a headache when I returned home and later found myself thanking God for my caring, though certainly flawed, home where I had grown up. It was clear that John's parents felt children had nothing of consequence to say and consequently didn't deserve a hearing either.

They are often separated from adults.

One day as our kids were growing up, I said to my wife after we had returned home from church, *"You know, Jackie, now that our kids are eight and thirteen, it would be possible that we would never sit together again in church as a family."* Tim, as the oldest, liked to sit with friends and Amy was old enough to be okay with other eight-year-olds.

Sunday School classes are invariably age-grouped, children's worship services take the place of worshipping with the adults, and even our choirs are graded. Wouldn't it be something to conduct a Sunday School elective containing nine- year-olds in a class studying the scriptures for 13 weeks WITH their parents? Some churches have made it work.

Every week boys and girls would see that they, too, are capable of learning and thinking about God and His Word right alongside big people. Children can be used in a similar way through participation in worship services, special programs, and service opportunities.

They are rarely asked to respond to life issues.

As young people mature, their ability to think more abstractly develops as well. While they used to know that $2+2 = 4$, they gradually learn that two apples plus two apples equals 4 apples. What was once a rote learning task became an applied idea.

In the same way we must remember that our young people, especially teenagers, have a developing, though often misused and misunderstood, sense of abstract thinking ability that adults must permit to be exercised. Asking our teens about tough questions may turn our faces red now and then, but our openness emits a clear message from us to them that their opinion matters.

Even seemingly skeptical questions from them about Christianity are fertile ground for letting an adolescent develop his mental abilities and gain a sense of his potential for thinking deeply about God NOW.

They feel inadequate.

I've attended and ministered at churches that have varied dramatically in size. They all have their strengths and weaknesses but there is one thing I particularly appreciated about the smaller ones. Children get to participate more.

Some churches are so committed to impressing people with their excellence that the average musician or the novice child or teen rarely gets to perform or participate. The message to them becomes clear, intended or not: *"You don't serve God publicly in this church until you are GOOD!"*

Yes, we do have a mandate from God to offer up excellent sacrifices of praise, and I heartily endorse seeking quality at every juncture of our programming. However, we can't keep saying to our kids that *someday* is the only time you can serve because we allow excellence to supersede any willingness to be involved.

I'm thankful that in our current church, many children, young people and older teens are regularly utilized to lead us in worship, perform dramatic roles, provide musical selections and challenge us spiritually.

One of the spiritual giants of Christian history possessed a father who was a serious-minded, severe, and industrious man who at times also drank too much. There were few pleasant memories and little joyousness of youth in the home. His mother, though not nearly so stern, was a willing accomplice nonetheless in demanding relentless work out of their young son.

He developed a strong dislike for his father and of his mother he states, "*She flogged me until I bled on account of a single nut.*" Anger was the standard emotion in young Martin Luther's household. How easily he might have been written off as an infidel, an unusable cog in the wheel of a dysfunctional household! And yet, as we all know, God took that troubled life and used him to change the course of history.

They're afraid to make a mistake.`

Our son played basketball early in his schooling for a coach who was a screamer. Yes, a screamer. The big joke in the stands was to see how long it took before we could watch the veins in the coach's neck start popping out. It was usually only a matter of minutes after the opening tip-off before the show started!

The tragic result of this coach's verbal barrages at his young ball players was that he placed terror in their souls, spewed out more horror if they messed up and then made them ultimately endure his wrath long after their error.

Make a mistake on the court, commit an errant pass, travelling or a missed assignment and you were out of the game and in some cases wouldn't play the rest of the night.

We parents longed for the day when just once he would pull one of the kids aside, lovingly but firmly show them their mistake and then say, "*Hey, go back in there and try it again.*" That never happened. You can imagine the effect this leader's uncontrollable flailings had on the young minds and egos of his young team.

As Christians, we need to do better than to expect perfection from our young people, but so often that's what we suggest by our actions. Not long after we moved to our first new home my son pierced my heart one day when he said tearfully, "*Dad, all you ever say to me lately is 'no'.*"

Oh sure, I had my excuses lined up in response, such as the fact that we had just moved to a new house, I had taken on a new job after fifteen years somewhere else and all that.

However, I am thankful that the Lord helped me recognize that I could easily have pushed Tim into thinking that he could never measure up or that he must someday meet all of my expectations.

"Sure, I'll try to please my dad," he might ponder," *someday when I'm good enough."* Or he might have spent the rest of his life desperately trying to come through for me, hoping that I might finally say to him," *Yes, you are acceptable."*

That night I merely said something like, "*Tim, I'm sorry and I have been terribly unfair to you. I'm going to work on saying 'yes' a whole lot more and explain more carefully when I have to say no. Please forgive me for being so unreasonable."*

Let's not forget our children, our teens, even our college-aged kids who, though still green, maturing, developing and imperfect, have also been given the privilege to be who they can be for God NOW.

If you are a teenager or young person, ask God what He wants to do in your life right NOW. Like King Josiah, Joseph, or the young kid with the loaves and the fish, God can use you in ways beyond what you could ever imagine!

Too Old To Serve?

I was attending a missions kids conference in Quito, Ecuador a number of years ago and had the opportunity through some friends to see several missions agencies in action. *Wycliffe, HCJB, Central American Mission* among others were at the time working diligently in that South American country.

As I toured the various offices, work places, hospitals and radio stations I noticed something which has intrigued and excited me ever since. There were people over sixty-five years of age serving everywhere.

These *gifted* saints of God were helping as secretaries, accountants, computer experts, video technicians, teachers, mechanics, carpenters and hundreds of other things.

The majority of them that I met were not career missionaries either. They had come to South America to begin a new chapter of service in their lives using the gifts and talents God had given them.

They were not about to give in to the *now-you're-retired-so-you're-not-needed anymore* thinking that so many of our elderly accept later in life. They wanted to be where the action is, doing something unique for God, learning a new language in some cases, seeing the world in the process. Some only stayed a few months, but the majority were there for at least a year, sometimes four or five.

You see the church needs to be thinking about the tremendous wealth of experience, talent and maturity our senior citizens can offer because they are already one of the biggest age groups in American society. We Baby-boomers are now at that time of our lives!

In fact, if our churches plan to release a significant amount of their ministry to the elderly, the world had better look out! Baby Boomers have never been ones to sit around and wait for things to happen! My hunch is that the Baby Boomer generation could fuel one of the largest short-term missions efforts in history!

Hopefully, more of us will think about being old like Ty Cobb, one of the greatest baseball players of all time, did. When Cobb was seventy, a reporter asked him, *"What do you think you'd hit if you were playing these days?"* Cobb, a lifetime .367 hitter, said, *"About .290, maybe .300."*

The reporter replied, "That's because of the travel, night games, the artificial turf, and all the new pitches like the slider, right?"

"No," said Cobb, *"it's because I'm seventy!"* I like that attitude!

You see, many seniors are caught up in the, *"Well, I'm simply going to wait around for Heaven,"* mentality and they just exist until the Lord calls them home. And yet, the apostle Paul never thought that way. Sure, he was anxious to be with the Lord and near the end struggled with staying on earth very much longer.

He told the Corinthians about how he groaned to have his dwelling place in Heaven. (II Corinthians 5:1ff) In Philippians he laments, *"But I am hard pressed from both directions, having the desire to depart and be with Christ, for that is very much better; yet to remain on in the flesh is more necessary for your sake."* Philippians 1: 23, 24)

Paul was going to live out his life for the glory of God to the very end! If the same can happen today, what are some jobs our super seniors might be well-suited to do in their later years?

Train Younger Believers

The apostle Paul wrote to his pastor/disciple friend Titus about the wonderful potential of the young learning from older when he wrote these words in Titus 2:1ff:

"But as for you, speak the things which are fitting for sound doctrine. Older men are to be temperate, dignified, sensible, sound in faith, in love, in perseverance. Older women, likewise, are to be reverent in their behavior, not malicious gossips, nor enslaved to much wine, teaching what is good, that they may encourage the young women to love their husbands, to love their children, to be sensible, pure workers at home, kind, being subject to their own husbands, that the word of God may not be dishonored."

God knows that the maturity, wisdom and big picture vantage-point of those living at retirement age has the potential to be one of the world's greatest object lessons for the younger generations of our churches and communities.

That dear elderly lady who teaches your son's 3rd grade class represents a life that speaks volumes because the children see the end product of the work of God in her life.

If you are fifty-something or more you remember when our country was fighting in the Vietnam War. As a high schooler I vividly recall who the calmest people were about our involvement in that war.

They were the senior citizens! Sure, they were concerned but most of them had already lived through World War I, World War II, and Korea so another war was hardly the worst thing that could happen to them. They have perspective, they see the big picture of life.

In a world that is constantly changing and often in turmoil we need the stability that comes from experience and our seniors have more of it than anyone. Seniors need to be on every team in our church, involved regularly with our young people both formally and informally, able to give testimony of what God has done and is still doing in their lives even after all these years.

Work in Full-time Christian Service

My experience in Ecuador was just a glimmer of what seniors could be doing in ministry both here in America and around the world. Thousands of opportunities lie waiting for a willing volunteer to come and help.

In terms of missions many seniors are financially stable enough that they would not need to raise near the support a young couple would have to collect to travel to another country. One of the largest areas of need is finding teachers to teach in schools for missionary children. One of our seniors has just returned from a trip to Russia and a work project in Belgium, all within a period of about six weeks! What a model she is to our younger families.

NOW!

Our missionary kids not only need to be taught curriculum but many would like to know what things are like in the United States so they can return on their furlough somewhat oriented to the ever- changing American scene. I can picture a group of high schoolers sitting at the feet of the newly-arrived senior citizen teacher asking scores of questions about teens and teen life back home!

Many of our recent retirees are skilled laborers, accountants, computer operators, engineers and mechanics. What an exciting challenge for a mature Christian to think of how to take his or her skills and refine them for use in a poorly developed country.

And what a blessing they would become for the missionary who so desperately wants to give his time to ministry and yet has been saddled with technical responsibilities he knows little or nothing about! Don't forget that this same senior could also become that missed *grandparent* that the missionary's children do not have because of the thousands of miles of separation from loved ones.

Work, however, is also available right here at home. Mission boards, youth agencies, Christian aide societies, crisis pregnancy centers and the like would all welcome volunteer (and perhaps paid) help from seniors who are willing to get involved. Church leaders need to begin to pave the way for senior involvement in ministry by developing contact lists and resource assistance and then secure a couple retirees to get things started.

Minister to other seniors

Who connects best to someone in the inner-city? A white, middle-class well-intentioned pastor or a native, minority trained in sharing the Gospel and discipleship? The answer is easy. The one who has lived there will minister best.

The same is true when it comes to working with senior citizens. Seniors have been there, so to speak, and understand the special needs of other seniors, so it only makes sense to give them a chance to work with their own people.

Perhaps the greatest concerns for retirees in America are boredom and loneliness. And yet seniors have the time and ability to help provide activities, fellowship and spiritual caring that so many need during the later years of life. Many pastors are simply overwhelmed because of the huge number of needs they must meet that they cannot possibly give their seniors all the personal attention that they want.

However, a committed and willing senior relating to his own peers would bring a richness and depth to caring for other seniors that the staff could never provide or match! Outreach opportunities also abound for seniors-aerobics classes, day trips, luncheons, hobby classes, Bible studies, you name it. A creative leader could attract seniors to a myriad of possible gatherings.

It's never too late. Today hasn't come and gone for the elderly in our churches and communities. Some years ago, a man over sixty was offered nearly $200,000 for a restaurant-motel-service station that he had spent his life building up. He turned the deal down because he loved what he was doing and was not ready to retire yet.

Two years later, at age sixty-five, he was broke with no income except his meager Social Security check each month. The state had built a new highway bypassing his business and he subsequently lost everything. Nevertheless, he didn't give up.

There was one thing he knew how to do. Fry chicken. In a battered old jalopy of a car, with only a pressure cooker and some specially prepared seasonings, he set out to sell his idea to other restaurants. Although it was tough going at first, by now most of us can recite the rest of the story.

A few years later everyone knew about him and was eating Kentucky Fried Chicken. Colonel Sanders was now a household name and his company an overwhelming success.

Are you a young person or a senior citizen? Don't let your age hinder you from meaningful, fruitful and exciting ministry for God. Let no one look down on your youthfulness, young people.

Let's review this challenge from Titus one more time:

"Older men are to be temperate, dignified, sensible, sound in faith, in love, in perseverance. Older women likewise are to be reverent in their behavior, not malicious gossips, nor enslaved to much wine, teaching what is good, that they may encourage the young women to love their husbands, to love their children." Does this sound like a life in neutral, senior friends?

Take the lead and find ways to spur many on to vital, active, exciting ministries for God. Think about organizing a missions trip or local service project that makes use of their special talents. What could you do? NOW?

Things to think about in chapter 10

What other things could the youth or seniors in your sphere of influence do to serve others   through the church?

What training do you think they might need before jumping in to a new ministry?

Who would you need to talk to in your setting to get approval to develop something with one of these age groups?

The Abused, Angry and Depressed
Chapter 11

*"We are a nation consumed by having . . . yet we are a society of
notoriously unhappy people; lonely, anxious, depressed, dependent."*
Tim Hansel

Have you seen it? There are hurting people in your
church, family, neighborhood, school and office.
Discouraged, despairing, frightened, abused, bitter for
hundreds of reasons due to an endless array of tough
circumstances. And yet, the church often sets them aside.

For many years, any form of weakness within the walls
of most evangelical congregations was considered
comparable to getting leprosy. Christ followers were
expected to always model joy and happiness, which
essentially meant to smile, even if you didn't feel like it.

A favorite maxim was, "*Let go and let God*," and you
could almost hear the strains of *Amazing Grace* playing in
the background as they said it.

Thankfully, much of Christendom has finally accepted
the fact that Christians, though forgiven of their sins, still
struggle (I John 3: 2,3). Life this side of Heaven is
imperfect. Families split, relationships end, and children
are mistreated.

Anger doesn't regularly get resolved before sundown
and many are overwhelmed by life's increasing demands

in current culture. Pastors, counselors and lay helpers have made strides in helping churches to become caring oases in the middle of the world's desert of phoniness and hopelessness.

However, if we're going to care for the troubled ones in our churches today, we must understand they also share a tendency toward *someday* living. Hurting people tend to find solace in their pain and as a result often remain trapped by their hurts instead of living responsibly NOW.

Potentially helpful options such as support groups or need-based Bible studies can still paralyze strugglers, leaving them mired in their angst. One woman recently told me about a ladies' book study she had just completed.

She said, "*Pastor, we had a terrific understanding of what our problem was, but we never seemed to get to the solution!*" Is it possible that her group was more comfortable entrenched in their pain than living without it?

Yes, there are scores of struggles that people we know encounter. However, I want to look at several situations which will show how the *Someday Syndrome* often reinforces those problems.

Keep in mind that each of the following conditions requires more attention than I can give it here. Others have written helpful and detailed treatments about each issue and those works are readily available.

My goal is to simply focus on the *someday* dynamic of each problem, hoping that the ideas from this brief look will help you or another person move forward with confidence and hope.

A recent University of Pennsylvania study estimates the number of children who are sexually abused each year is nearly 244,000, most often middle-class children. Recently Olympic gymnasts have revealed years of abuse they suffered as young athletes and the fear that covered their deep dark secret

A friend of mine took a new position in a church in the Midwest, thinking he was leaving the evils of the big city, only to have his toddler son sexually abused in the church nursery of his conservative, evangelical church in the Bible Belt.

As I write, the Catholic church in America continues to face monumental repercussions as more and more of its priests are accused and convicted of pedophilia. The church will be reeling for decades because of this evil perpetrated by these once trusted leaders.

Many of the abused don't even know or recall that they were abused. I remember some years ago having a counseling session with a young woman who after several sessions blurted out, "*Oh my god, my father was abusing me!*" For years her mind had hidden the reality of what her daddy had been doing to her each week.

However, it's important to remember that when people do recall their abuse, physical, sexual, verbal or emotional, they usually encounter a powerful urge to avoid dealing with it in a productive or helpful manner. They'd rather run somewhere else.

An inner voice keeps telling them, "Don't say anything to anyone right now. This isn't the time. Maybe someday you will be able to reveal your mistreatment and the resulting feelings, but think of the mess you will avoid if you keep quiet."

Why do the abused stay silent?

Fear

We've seen this emotion before, haven't we? But abused people are often afraid of something different, of what others will say or think. They shudder at the thought that they could be seen as dirty or unclean. They are terrified that no one will believe them and that they will be rejected by those who now love them.

Sadly, the sexually abused typically avoid genuine intimacy with their spouse, if married, or with others who they might enjoy relationship with in everyday life. The potential good that was present, even in their destructive relationship such as being loved, the closeness of a father, the touch of someone who cared. All that has now been cast aside with the memory of the actual abuse.

Intimacy is but a foggy dream in their *someday* file, which in their minds could never, ever again be a reality for them. The thought of closeness with someone only invites more terror and panic. The only option left in their minds is a hasty retreat to their prison of silence and loneliness. At least it is safe there. Or so it seems.

But the abused don't need to live in a someday world either. Yes, the abuser may never get her just due in this life. The movie can't be started over and played again with a different ending. The pain may I n fact increase as the abuse is re-visited.

However, a person who has been abused can learn to embrace the life-changing truth that there is no event, no circumstance, no failure that has the power to own us Consider II Corinthians 4:4ff and its perspective on battling even the worst of situations.

"But we have this treasure in jars of clay, to show that this all surpassing power is from God and not from us; we are hard pressed on every side, but not crushed; perplexed, but not in despair; persecuted, but not abandoned; struck down, but not destroyed . . . so that the life of Jesus may also be revealed in our body."

Later in the same chapter, Paul adds verse 16, *"Therefore, we do not lose heart. Though outwardly we are wasting away, yet inwardly we are being renewed day by day."*

Are his comments merely the ramblings of a fair-weather preacher? No, they are the God-breathed utterings through Paul of one who endured the worst of beatings, torture and significant abuse. He knew that healing was often a slow process but reminds us that we can move on – NOW!

If you have been abused, you are not dirty in God's eyes! You are valuable, have great worth because of Christ's death for you, and possess incredible potential to be used by God to make a difference in your world. *You don't need to succumb to paralysis because of your past.*

Your healing process may be painfully slow but you can do something anyway. Perhaps the first step will be to tell someone you can trust about the abuse.

Don't hide in the someday world of excuses. Tell a trusted friend, talk with a wise confidante who will help you face your past hurts and point you towards the God who loves you.

You can also *begin to enjoy part of the fruit of relationship* with others. Spend more time with people. Relish it. Learn to laugh again. Go to someone who can help you on the long road to full recovery and healing. Get started! Nothing is stopping you. God has promised to be with you every step of the way!

Someday And The Angry.

You might not know it, but angry people are nearby, too. They may actually be a little more noticeable because anger has a way of leaking out, even from highly controlled people.

They drive cars, go to their kids' games and lead big corporations. And they are not just those who are a little ticked off about something that happened while they were getting ready for church. No, they are often people who are raging about LIFE!

Just today, my wife Jackie had a driver in a pickup truck literally scream at her for him having to switch lanes to pass her.

Maybe you're one of those people. Nice, smiling, gracious on the outside, an island unto yourself, yet furious at the core of your being. You may not even comprehend what ignites your outbursts in the first place, but you know full well that your emotional pot is boiling most of the time.

Unfortunately, the smallest irritations evoke harsh words that plummet deep into the souls of their spouses, children, friends and neighbors. People tend to tiptoe around these raging bulls fearful of setting off the nitroglycerin inside them and enduring the hot lava of their verbal volcano.

Time Magazine reported on the rage which plagued news mogul Ted Turner for so many years. In his sailing days he was rarely home. When he did spend time with his family, says his eldest son Teddy, he behaved as though "*kids were a necessary evil.*"

He forbade crying, snapped at the slightest imperfection and ran his weekends at his South Carolina plantation on a militaristic schedule of dawn-to-dusk hunting.

Teddy remembers the canoe trip he and his two brothers took with their father when Teddy was about 11. Turner, he says, "*Yelled and screamed the whole time. It was a nightmare . . . .*"

As a skipper, he occasionally struck crew members who made mistakes. At the office his bursts of violence were verbal, but almost all his top executives say they have felt them."

Anger seems to be even more rampant than ever even in some of the most unusual settings though rage isn't exactly a new commodity.

Anger in High Gear

You may be thinking at this point, "*Okay, it's been quite easy to see the thinking in the people you've discussed up until now, but what's the someday mentality for an angry person? Isn't he or she just trying to get everything their way NOW and not worrying about tomorrow?*"]

And on the surface, you're right! Angry people are only thinking about NOW in one sense. However, in reality they are also demanding that things in the future or the world of the impossible must happen today! Let me give you a personal example.

Remember my discussion about how unmechanical I've always been? When I was first married I believed with all my heart that to be a good husband I must be a *fixer*. So naturally I would go out into my garage and attempt to repair or do some routine (unfortunately not routine to me) maintenance on my car.

However, when I found myself incapable of doing the work I didn't simply retreat into the house, call a friend for help or even take it to a mechanic. My blood began to boil! In fact, I would have been horribly embarrassed for someone to see or hear the fury of my rage in that garage.

Why was I so mad? Just because the car didn't get fixed? No way! I was demanding that I be able to be mechanical (or at least appear to be) at that very moment, so that I could maintain my role as a man, husband and fixer. In my mind, *someday* I was going to be a mechanic and that *someday* was going to be NOW!! But it wasn't happening.

Angry people are typically demanding people who believe that things, friends, actions, accomplishments must all help meet the goal of getting their worth back.

Unfortunately, what they usually demand is neither necessary nor in their control most of the time. My lack of skills in auto repair was not something I could manipulate. I never had the training for it and God chose not to give me the enthusiasm to learn more.

But more importantly, I had to accept that I didn't need to be mechanical to be a responsible, loving, caring husband to my wife or a happy, fulfilled man in God's family.

My anger would only subside when my mind began to comprehend that I could go on in spite of my inabilities and still be the person God wanted me to be. God particularly liked to remind me of this each time I moved because He placed next door to or across the street from various handymen who really knew what they were doing.

I still struggle going to ask the Jeffs, Keiths or Charlies of the world, wondering if this time they will say, "*Oh, here comes Mr. Klutz again! What's broken now?*" But more and more I am enjoying taking responsibility to have our home needs met, even if I am not the one responsible to do the work.

The Importance of Control

If you're old enough to have experienced it, you will ever forget the horror of Columbine, right? Sadly, similar incidents continue to occur throughout our country.

In Colorado during that horrible tragedy, young, innocent students were executed in front of their peers by two rage-filled, rejected teen boys. Apparently, their anger seethed for months as they meticulously laid their plans to get even with those they believed pushed them away.

But imagine their glee when instead of others walking by mocking them they could cause those same enemies to cower under tables and in doorways before fatally shooting many of them. That scene has tragically been replayed over and over in schools, churches and neighborhoods ever since.

Thankfully, the people we know are probably not this despairing. But some very angry Christians may be the hardest workers you know. Many of the power-brokers in our culture today are seething inside.

Some of our most gifted and talented people-helpers are the most vengeful. Angry believers tend to rise to the top. Leadership and power, and the apparent control they provide, become anesthetics, dulling the pain that results when life doesn't give us what we want.

If a person is in a job where he doesn't get much respect, he will often demand it at church. If a wife doesn't find intimacy in her marriage, she may seek it from those she is close to spiritually. When people don't get what they think they must have, anger is often the responses. You see, anger is a wonderfully pragmatic form of control!

Have you ever been in a room where someone literally blows their cork? What happens? The whole place gets unnervingly quiet, doesn't it? The rage worked! It forced everyone else to succumb to the screamer's outburst. No one dared respond for fear of unleashing even more venom towards themselves or others.

As a consequence, anger is a very potent form of the *Someday Syndrome*. The thinking often goes, "*Someday I will have _____, so in the meantime, I will demand it from you NOW!*" In my case, I was sure that I could one day be quite handy, so I was incensed when I could not perform adequately right then.

A son is convinced that he WILL get his father's respect, and yet when at forty years of age his father continues to degrade his occupation or ministry, the man's rage still boils.

Angry people think they are in control of life while in reality *life controls them*! Not only do they miss out on the joys of everyday living but their energy and enthusiasm for anything enjoyable is sapped by their intense fury, internal or external.

Letting It All Out

Of course, *NOW* people do get angry at times, too. But *NOW* people know what to do with their anger. They recognize it when it surfaces, see it for what it is and deal with it appropriately. They can tell the difference between righteous and unrighteous anger.

Think of your anger as the air in a balloon. Basically, there are three ways to get it out. First, you could pop the balloon with a sharp object but the result is probably an explosion. Second, you can let go of the end of the balloon like you did when you were a kid. The balloon flies wildly around the room landing somewhere in a heap. Or, you can let the air seep out a little bit at a time.

When it comes to anger, the first two methods cause needless hurt and pain. Exploding only provides temporary control, and in the end damage can be done. Our blood pressure rises and we risk losing relationships we once coveted.

Flying out of control like the second balloon usually makes problems worse, can injure us and we still ache inside, landing in an emotional pile. At the same time, we may also be destroying good parts of relationship that we already enjoy.

But the person freed from the *Someday Syndrome* is able to release his or her anger, illegitimate or not, in a chosen, appropriate fashion. By doing so they can more easily recognize the selfishness that lies behind their rage while expressing it appropriately, no longer demanding a specific outcome.

The person who loses a job may be deeply saddened and feel justified in discussing the firing at length with his boss, even expressing injustices if they are valid. However, if he realizes that his worth was never wrapped up in his job to begin with, he will enjoy a refreshing liberty to move on, and with God's help, to find work elsewhere.

He may hope for his boss' recognition and appreciation, but he won't need to require it anymore to live a fulfilled and satisfied life. In the meantime, he can enjoy life as it is *NOW*, not having to wait for the *someday* of a new job to be happy again.

The Apostle Paul speaks about anger several times. In Colossians 3:8 he writes, *"But now you must rid yourselves of all such things as these: anger, rage, malice, slander and filthy language."* In the original language, to put aside implied *to lay down,* to not let it stand anymore or have an influence. As we become people of *NOW*, God can help us become

less angry while demanding less that things work out on
our terms.

At times, when I have been angry with my children,
my emotional response was not due to their actions for
the most part. Often, I was furious because I was
requiring that my children perform in such and such a
way so that I would not be embarrassed.

When I was pastoring, I found the temptation to do
the same with people in my congregation even more
enticing. I didn't want them to embarrass me! *Please be
kind, please grow in your faith, please come to church regularly.*

But fortunately, I am learning that my children (or
wife, or clients, or church constituency) do not have to
meet my behavioral expectations for me to find joy. I'm
sad when they do not, but I don't have to demand that
they change.

I am free to respond lovingly, biblically and
appropriately, doing what is best for them at the time.

Are you often a kettle of water waiting to boil over?
Ask yourself what somedays you are demanding right
then. Bring them to God, talk them over with someone
who will listen and leave them before the Lord.

Christ died so that you and I could let go of what we
demand and substitute what God provides to meet our
deepest needs. As a result, you and I can walk away from
the chains of our anger and begin to enjoy FREEDOM in
Christ.

Someday And The Depressed

It appears in a wide array of forms and degrees. What
starts out as a now and then feeling may evolve into an
overwhelming dread about life, at least for some. A
percentage of its victims function somewhat normally
within their daily routines, while others feel they literally
cannot get out of bed in the morning.

Depression has, at least in some circles, become the new catch-all word for scores of emotional and even physical maladies, resulting from job loss, marital difficulties, family strife, and other negative situations. The worst scenario often culminates in suicide. Recent research suggests that one fourth of top-level executives go through depression at some point in their careers.

Psychologists indicate that Americans are more likely to suffer from clinical depression than at any time in history. Depression knows few age boundaries any more. Sadly, more and more teenagers have been diagnosed as clinically depressed, while the teen suicide rate remains alarmingly high.

Of course, there are forms of depression that are largely out of our control, where chemical imbalances within the brain take charge and depression is the unfortunate result. Many women each month suffer varying degrees of depression during their menstrual cycles.

These types of episodes should naturally be dealt with under the watchful care of a physician. However, non-organically induced depression also has a component in *Someday* living that many of us would benefit from if we understood it better. That element is UNMET and IMPOSSIBLE EXPECTATIONS.

When Hope Is Gone

Philip was a fifty-two-year-old executive for a successful computer firm, having served the company faithfully for 22 years. He was around during the days when laptops and PCs were not even being thought of yet. Hand calculators that could add, subtract, multiply and divide and do square roots were the new rage then costing a mere sixty-five dollars!

Computers for the average person were not available when Phil was growing up, however. He made his mark in school with his keen mathematical mind and natural abilities in problem solving and analysis. He had some modest success playing trumpet in the school band and even considered pursuing music at one point.

His intellect won out, though, with counselors and teachers urging him on to consider engineering, architecture, and other technical fields. He also found himself relishing the positive attention he received from his school achievements, especially since living at home was a much different story.

Phil's dad had little tolerance for a kid who wasn't a jock. *"If you can't play football, Phil, then at least try out for baseball, or track or something,"* his Dad would often bellow. Phil recalls the painful memories of being hit in the face with a ball, having to run with dad for miles at a time, only to hear, *"C'mon, Phil, move it, move it, move it!"*

At times he wondered if joining the Marines wouldn't be like a vacation. He had heard regularly about his father's athletic accomplishments, making dad sound like he should have been in the Olympics or something!

The one time Phil ever received an award, *Top Math Student in the Senior Class,* dad and mom didn't show up. It seems they had an office party to attend.

Phil didn't know it at the time, but somewhere around the beginning of his college years, in the late fifties, he embarked on a mission of sorts, a quest that would take the large part of his emotional energy, and guide most of his future decisions.

His challenge? To someday make his father proud of him! Phil obtained his college degree in electrical engineering and soon became enthralled with computers as they evolved within the business and corporate scene.

His problem solving and analytical skills were tailor-made for the rapid-fire technological changes of the 60's and 70's. He skyrocketed to near the top of a prestigious computer firm and received his MBA just two years later .

Sadly, his relationship with his father remained strained. Instead of being proud of Philip, dad would be candidly blunt. Nothing was ever good enough. Phil's children were being deprived, he said, because they don't have a dad who can throw the ball around with them. The few times his father ever asked Phil to do something with him, the agenda was either tennis, a ballgame or running.

Although he hated his father at times, Phil also longed for the day when Dad would just once say, "*Son, I'm proud of you.*"

Phil remembers one faint hope for that wish. His company had agreed to help pay for him to pursue his doctorate degree in computer engineering, a move which would not only add prestige for him and his company, but allow him to teach part-time at the university. It would be a solid public relations move, too, and would assist his company tap into the college market.

No one in Phil's family had ever come close to a Ph.D. Dad certainly knew that and Phil thought, "*Hey, getting a doctorate will be a little bit like winning the Super Bowl, won't it? This will surely make an impression on dad.*"

Unfortunately, Phil's hopes were soon dashed on the rocks of circumstances. His wife was diagnosed with a slow-moving cancer, one which required lengthy and costly treatments, not all covered by insurance. He loved his wife, Terry, and sensed an important obligation to be with her as much as possible.

Several nights each week attending classes, plus the additional expenses over and above the company's contribution, were out of the question now.

Phil became depressed, unmotivated to get up for work, tired much of the time from fitful nights of sleep, and disinterested in his company's new projects. Past hobbies like reading, walks with Terry and crossword puzzles were un-appealing now. He watched TV more than ever, but actually enjoyed it less and less. At times he could be found crying for no apparent reason.

Phil's depression was his response to a *someday* that was now out of reach. "*Someday, my dad will appreciate me!*" his heart cried. "*I'll show him that I matter.*" But in reality, Phil now faced the possibility that his quest for dad's love would never be consummated.

Actually, this possibility had existed all along Phil's life path - he just didn't know it. Even if he had attained the new degree, his father may still have rejected him!

Depression became a safe place to hide. When someone is depressed, people cannot expect them to function as normal people with responsibilities, tasks, and demands on their lives. The depressed person wants no more requirements on him that cannot be fulfilled so he chooses to stay in the pit of personal darkness and loneliness, horrible though it may be.

Severely depressed people move very little. They do not believe that they can perform normally anymore, which is a lie. They fear the hurt of facing the real world again, where they must live with one or more impossible goals that can never be attained.

If Phil leaves his depression he will have to function in this everyday world, knowing that his father has still not accepted him and perhaps never will. And because Phil believes that his father's opinion of him is essential for happiness, putting life on hold using his depression is his answer. The *Someday Syndrome* has paralyzed another victim!

Scores of impossible somedays plague Christians everywhere. Interestingly, many individuals succumb to the impossible during the mid-life crisis years as they begin to realize that there are numerous goals, plans, hopes and dreams that won't come to pass.

They have fought and fought, believing that someday things would be different, but the hourglass sand is running out. There is no more time to make any of their dreams happen.

Let me suggest a few potential unmet goals that could still paralyze us. Our list may differ in things we would add or subtract but these should get you started in thinking about their impact.

I didn't:

Please my dad
Get my daughter to love me
Make the team
Have children
Write a book
Receive an "A"
Finish my education
Get accepted to med school
Receive forgiveness
Get married
Stay healthy`

When these and other beliefs take hold, our depression can serve as a giant STOP sign that says, "I can't go on anymore. If my expectations and demands can't be met, I won't be able to function any longer."

For years the depressed person has looked at the carrot of false hopes being dangled in front of their eyes. confident that someday they would catch it and life would taste wonderful. It is such a tragedy to see these illusive somedays given the power to bring to stop talented, gifted, usable people, keeping them from dynamic change and effective service that God made them for!

It would be insensitive, of course, and a huge lie to tell depressed people that unmet hopes, dreams, longings and desires should not hurt. The truth is they are painful most of the time!

Who wouldn't be sad if they had Phil's dad as a parent? Who wouldn't be disappointed and discouraged if they couldn't get into medical school or were turned down for a seemingly fantastic job opportunity?

But consider again the apostle Paul's words in II Corinthians 4: *"We are afflicted, but not crushed; perplexed, but not despairing; persecuted, but not forsaken; struck down, but not destroyed."*

Paul knew that serving Jesus could be very difficult and even traumatic. Later in II Corinthians he describes in greater detail the personal struggles he faced throughout his ministry. Even so, nothing in this world was capable of stopping Paul from his commitment to Christ.

The same universal truth is still true for each of us. NOTHING deserves the right to impede our progress to become more like Jesus.

In the center of struggle, the emotions of a *NOW* person will lean towards concern, sadness, disappointment, even righteous anger. Each of these responses is PRODUCTIVE, allowing a person to move onward, even though they may be temporarily slowed.

In contrast, the *someday* individual tends to respond with despair, rage, panic and devastation, all emotional dead-ends.

In their helpful, now classic writing on depression, Meier and Minrith reminded us that *happiness is a choice.* However, remember it's a choice based on a clear understanding of where our love and worth are really found and that's in God Himself! You or someone you know who is depressed can choose to behave differently.

To begin, though, you will need to have some confidence that your worth as a person is still intact, despite the fact that your impossible expectations were never fulfilled.

George Sand, (a pseudonym to cover "her" real name), was a famous 19th century French novelist. At age forty-two, however, she was broken and depressed, her personal life a shambles while having endured intense personal criticism from her beloved French people.

Although not a Christian, in her own humanity she was soon able to say with confidence, *"Henceforth, I shall accept what I am and what I am not. With my limitations and my gifts, I shall go on using life as long as I am in this world and afterwards. Not to use life- that alone is death."*
Following her "rebirth" she went on to write another fifty plays and novels!

Consider starting with one small act, one which could affirm what you now know in your mind. Take Phil's situation again for a moment. In spite of his sadness over his lost chance to win his dad's admiration, Phil continues to be the most loving husband to his especially needy wife.

He is free to go on loving his father in spite of his continued rejections. Perhaps most importantly, he is free to come before God, broken, hurting, and dejected, to experience His loving comfort, care and love.

Like David, in Psalm 22, Phil can turn to the Lord in his most trying of circumstances. In verses 11-18, we hear David's passionate portrayal of his depressed state, which God miraculously used as a prophetic picture of the crucifixion. Listen to some of David's despairing lament:

Be not far from me, for trouble is near; for there is none to help. . . I am poured out like water, and all my bones are out of joint; My heart is like wax; It is melted within me. . . . They have pierced my hands and my feet. I can count all my bones."

And yet, in the center of his overwhelming darkness, David is still able to praise God and choose to function, even if only in a simple way. Listen to his response later in the chapter:

"But Thou, O Lord, be not far off . . . I will tell of Thy name to my brethren; In the midst of the assembly I will praise Thee. You who fear the Lord, praise Him . . . For He has not despised or abhorred the affliction of the afflicted; Neither has He hidden His face from him. But when he cried to Him for help, He heard. . . The afflicted shall hear and be satisfied. (22: 19 - 26)

Are you depressed? What is it that you feel you must have which now appears will never come? Identify it, bring it before God, let Him help reveal it to you even if you don't see it right now.

Next, confess to God that you have been requiring that some event, circumstance or feeling must happen for you to be fulfilled and satisfied. Tell God you now realize that this demand on your part has been wrong and ultimately sinful. Ask Him for forgiveness and help in renewing your mind (Romans 12: 2) each day to think in a radically new way about where true life is found.

Express your sadness to the Lord, and even to others, over those things you longed for, but which never happened. Remember, your wanting to be loved and valued is God-given and should never be discounted.

You have the opportunity to experience freedom once again to live life no longer demanding that other people provide what only God can give you. Ask God to help you little by little to act, to re-discover your ability to function in the real world as you are. Let God's unseen rope of love hold you and then enjoy the ride.

Slowly your depression will subside and the peace of God will begin to take its place. In the next chapter I'll look at one more group of *someday* people who I call, *Unlikely Heroes: The Average, Abnormal and Antagonistic.*

Things to Think About In Chapter 11

What part of your troubled past is keeping you from being who you could be? What in this chapter resonated with you that could help free you from that trap?

Who do you know who has struggled with something similar? Consider calling them and asking them if they would share things with you sometime that helped them over that hurdle.

Go to Amazon.com and get my book, *Never Quit Climbing*, in paperback or eBook form. Read it slowly over the next few weeks and add insights from it that could also move you forward and up this mountain you're facing.

Consider talking to a professional about your past challenges in light of what you've read in the first eleven chapters

AVERAGE, ABNORMAL, ANTAGONISTIC
CHAPTER 12

"If I had any luck at all, it would be bad."
Anthony Young (Pitcher for the New York Mets
who lost twenty-seven games in a row).

Doug was the kind of student most teachers never forget. Not because he was always bad but because he usually had you on edge! You never knew what he might try next. One moment he was answering your question with deep insight and analysis. The next second, he was daydreaming, annoying the nearest student with his silly antics or doodling in his notebook with the intensity of a Rembrandt.

As his teacher, I would at times be angry at Doug while on other occasions he made me laugh. I remember wanting most though to somehow get through to him, to help him see how much potential he had to be used by God, that he mattered and could make a difference in his world. Sadly, Doug left our school after graduation and as far as I knew he was no different than when he came to us some 6 years before.

One day, several years later, I was working hard behind my desk in my counseling office when I heard an unannounced voice blurt out, *"Hey, Mr. Sinclair, how are you doing?"* I looked up only to find myself staring into the eyes of Doug, that long-lost former student. I found myself confused for a moment, struggling to recall who he was, sure that his name was somewhere in my memory bank.

Doug, thankfully, bailed me out before my mind finished its sluggish computing and continued, "*Remember me, Doug Jenkins?*" (Not his real name)

"*I sure do,*" I replied, my mind scrambling for some innocuous thing I might say next. Concurrently I was starting to remember his classroom antics that were some of my most challenging moments as a teacher.

My discomfort, however, was short-lived as Doug began to relate the changes that had taken place in his life during the last several years.

Not long after graduation Doug came to know Christ, subsequently attended a Christian college and had just began a youth ministry in a nearby church. As he finished his update, he quite humbly said, "*I just thought you would like to know.*"

Like to know? Was he kidding? I was thrilled! Gone was the frivolous, "*Who cares?*", attitude I had experienced just years before. The immature, young man who flip-flopped through classes like a fish on land had matured. A caring, committed disciple stood there before me, grinning with his new sense of accomplishment.

With a tear in my eye, I could only stand, grasp his hand firmly and say, "*Doug, you don't know how happy I am. I'm proud of you!*" We talked for a while, but then he had to leave. I am guessing he was anxious to tell his story to others who would be blessed as I had been.

Since that day, I have witnessed many other unlikely candidates for God service turned away from lives of what seemed to be inability, incompetence and even excessive pride to become avid followers of Jesus.

Some years ago, I happened upon the *700 Club* while doing my manly duty of flipping through the channels on the remote. The program's special guest was the late

Charles Colson, who became an eloquent spokesman for Christ through his years with *Prison Fellowship Ministry*. Charles Colson lived much of his life deceiving others and power brokering in the political battlefields of Washington.

Anyone over fifty certainly remembers Colson's role in the Watergate scandal during the Nixon years and his subsequent sentencing and jail term. And yet, God in his sovereignty took Charles Colson's broken life and multiplied it just as he did the loaves and the fishes of the little boy in the feeding of the 5000. Years after his passing, Colson's influence and wisdom continue to impact thousands of lives.

Unfortunately, many of the potential Charles Colsons and Dougs are ignored by schools, churches and even their own families because of *someday* thinking. *"If only my Tom would apply himself and get better grades, he could amount to something,"* a frustrated parent laments. In other words, in their minds, Tom will never be successful. He doesn't even care about school.

Young parents today now force their preschoolers into gymnastics and advanced reading programs to avoid the stigma of being average. High schoolers are involved in music, sports and other learning programs year-round now because they can't keep up with the competition if they take time off.

"If Jane just didn't have so many problems, she could really be a wonderful girl," a discouraged counselor says with a sigh. What she means is that Jane would really be important if she weren't abnormal.

Personal issues (see the last chapter) have become the excuse of millions to either be excused or exonerate themselves from effective and normal (what is that anyway?) living.

Many Christians have also bought into the world's destructive philosophies that espouse beauty, intellect and physical strength as the tickets to success. Have you watched any awards programs lately? You rarely see an unattractive movie or music star, do you?

Finally, there are those who are antagonistic towards Christian things or God Himself. They may be the spouse of an attendee at our church, victims of past personal entanglements and misunderstandings, members of highly dysfunctional families, children of fallen church leaders and the like.

Although similar in many ways to the angry people we referred to in the last chapter, these individuals have transferred their anger for a variety of reasons to God, the church and Christians in general.

And sadly, those of us who know them find it easy to relegate them to a spiritual Purgatory, disqualifying them from any significant place in our world or the life of the church. People who are outwardly angry at parents, bosses and the world can be quickly added to our rejection pile.

Of course, there are millions of unlikely heroes that are ignored or rejected for other reasons, but I believe the average, abnormal, and antagonistic labels account for the majority of cases of people left untouched, unchanged and thereby passed over as important to the rest of society.

Perhaps you know someone in one of these categories or sense you have been labeled this way by others or yourself. Then hopefully this chapter will help you to step out of the quicksand of immobility and begin to see yourself and others as God sees, yes, with His eyes.

Remember, God is the one who decides on *normal!* He is more in the business of exceptional and special anyway.

Average Joe's and Josephine's

Not so many years ago, scoring around the mean on a test was considered normal. A grade of 'C' meant you were doing OK for someone your age. In recent years, however, average has come to imply being mundane, unexceptional and clearly less than desirable.

A 'C' grade in college is thought to be a failure to many, while in graduate school a grade lower than a "B" can signal the end of a career.

And yet some of God's foremost champions were barely average citizens prior to the Lord's holy touch upon their lives. What if these future superstars would have succumbed to the *Someday Syndrome* using the excuse, "*I just don't have enough talent for God to use me significantly?*" What if they had been overlooked by God because they weren't the cream of the intellectual crop?

Churches today cry for help as they seek to add essential ministries that would impact their community and enrich their body of believers. But only a small percentage of church attenders regularly volunteer. Volunteering in the church has dropped 7% in the last decade.

Could it be that many choose not to serve because they cannot envision themselves as talented or spiritual enough, especially compared to the pastoral staff and church leadership? Unfortunately, churches that have refused to change over time and utilize new technologies, art, drama, and the like have simply added to the lack of opportunities for the average person to serve.

Go from I never to NOW!

Remember Moses, God's chosen leader to guide the people out of Egypt through their forty-year wanderings to the gateway of the promised land? Although he experienced a rather remarkable escape from death shortly after his birth, Moses clearly admitted his own average-ness when God summoned him for a place in leadership.

In fact, at the time of Moses' encounter with God, Moses was tending his father-in-law's flock of sheep in the middle of the desert. It took no less than a burning bush to capture his attention!

Nonetheless, once Moses heard the magnitude of the assignment God had for him, he quickly deferred to his weaknesses, especially his poor communication skills. *"What if they don't believe in me or listen to me and say, 'The Lord did not appear to you'?"*

Several miraculous signs from God, including a stick turned into a snake and a hand covered with leprosy, should have convinced Moses that he was capable while in God's hands. Instead, God's chosen servant succumbs to his inabilities once more. *"O Lord, I have never been eloquent, neither in the past nor since you have spoken to your servant. I am slow of speech and tongue."* (Exodus 4:10)

Even Moses' own words express his bondage to his perceived incompetency. He says, "*I have never . . . .*"

What does that tell us? Proverbs speaks of the tongue having the power of life and death and here Moses speaks three words of death that have killed more effective ministry for Christ than perhaps any others, "*I have never . . . .*"

Perhaps you are saying in your mind right now, "I have never . . . taught a Sunday School class . . . witnessed to a neighbor . . lobbied in Washington . . . taken a seminary class . . . led a team . . .helped out in worship" or one of a thousand other challenges that God may ask you to undertake. You may be responding as Moses did by giving in to your sensed incompetence instead of trusting in the greatness of God?

With Moses, God finally became angry following his final appeal to God to please send someone else. God wanted Moses to rely on Him, no more, no less. As the now well-worn phrase says, God was not interested in Moses' ability as much as his availability.

Average people are forced to depend on God for their results. Moses was about to learn that lesson well and afterward became one of the greatest biblical leaders of all time.

Average people in God's hands with a challenge from Him can accomplish so much! An average person + God's power = extraordinary results.

John Stephen Akhwari was still running at 7:00pm on October 20, 1968 while only a few thousand spectators remained in the Mexico City Olympic Stadium.

The last of the marathoners had finished, many dehydrated, exhausted and being carried away on stretchers. Most of the spectators were preparing to leave when they suddenly heard the sounds of sirens and turned their eyes quickly towards the main entrance.

There they saw a lone figure, John Stephen Akhwari, in his Tanzanian running garb, hobbling around the last lap of the 400-meter track. His leg was bleeding and bandaged from a serious fall and he grimaced with each succeeding step. The spectators cheered and applauded him until he was well beyond the finish line.

When asked why he hadn't quit he responded, *"My country did not send me 7000 miles to start the race. They sent me 7000 miles to finish it."* John Akhwari wasn't about to be stopped because he was less than average!

God's people mustn't quit either! What must average people do to become one of God's heroes? Pray and ask God to give you a vision for a task bigger than you are.

God may give us a big or small role. Perhaps He is speaking to you about missions. That implies raising funds, possibly learning a language, leaving your family and living in a new community. Just the thought of all those requirements would be overwhelming to even the most capable of people.

Let me suggest that you begin by allowing God to guide you into a first step opportunity, one which could give you a taste of serving others. Many people from churches I've pastored went out of their area or overseas to minister to others through short-term trips.

Not only did they learn about what their future might hold or not, they rarely returned the same! There were many benefits in going.

I think of John who has been a hard worker most of his life, good with his hands and eager to please. But only recently has he crossed the bridge so to speak to know Christ.

He first got started serving by building props for some of our major productions. He did so with abandon but still seemed to only feel comfortable being in his element. Relating to and getting to know others wasn't his thing. Talking about spiritual things or ministry wasn't normal for him.

But one year he took his first airplane trip – to Kosovo – on a short-term missions trip. He had to raise funds and couldn't imagine how he could come up with the money. Nonetheless, he raised what he needed and had money left over!

We typically like to keep ourselves just sufficient enough most of the time that we really do not need any supernatural help from God! But we will never know the greatness of God's power if we won't put ourselves in a position to require it.

For several summers during my career in education I attended seminary in Dallas which necessitated our renting a home there and finding someone to live in our home for ten weeks.

Because we lived in suburban Detroit, hardly the vacation capital of the world, it was usually difficult to find someone to rent our house for such a short time. Every summer we would come within days of having to leave for Dallas and still not have a renter, and yet God always came through for us, even when we thought all options were gone.

He also provided the money for us to go, houses to rent in Dallas and even a job cleaning pools one year to help pay the bills. We realized that God doesn't always work things out our way and sometimes He allows us to be stretched beyond what we think we can do even if we're just *average*.

Jackie and I look back on that time as one of our life turning points that moved us to trust Him more and take on the challenges He gave us.

Take inventory of your skills and weaknesses.

If you will be honest about both areas, you will see that you do have much to offer as you rely on God and others to see your project through. I've had to regularly keep facing my mechanical inabilities and instead tackle projects that would not require that skill in me! What a relief to let go of something that I never needed to excel in anyway.

Remember earlier when I talked about Colonel Sanders. There's more to the story. As a sixty-something man he was offered almost $200,000 for a restaurant-motel-service station business that he'd spent his life building up. But he turned the offer down citing that he truly loved his business and was not about to retire yet.

Two years later, at age sixty-five, he was destitute with nothing to live on but a small Social Security check each month. You see the state had built a new highway causing traffic to bypass his once-thriving business and he lost everything.

But instead of giving up, he began to ponder what he was good at. He knew of just one thing - he could cook fried chicken. He wondered if anyone else would buy his knowledge and expertise. He set off to find out in a junky, old car, a pressure cooker and a supply of his special-recipe flour.

Some nights he even slept in his car but in only a few short years he had built a nationwide restaurant chain now known as Kentucky Fried Chicken. God has gifted us all with skills that we can use for his glory and to expand His kingdom.

It seems likely that the lists of spiritual gifts in the New Testament (see Romans 12, Ephesians 4, I Corinthians 12, and I Peter 4) are varied, numerous and incomplete because God has a legion of gifts and talents that he has placed throughout his people. He is waiting for us to ask for His touch to bring those gifts to light.

Carefully read and pray through these lists and see what gift or gifts God has given you to make a difference in the world around you and His church! Ask for help.

If a task is bigger than we are then it makes sense that we can't complete it alone. Delegate portions of the process to others, call on those who are already serving who can assist you along the way.

Find someone who will be a teammate and soulmate with you. Later in Moses' ministry, his father-in-law Jethro wisely encouraged him to select others to help him solve the problems of the people. Today we call Moses' problem *burn out* and we need to do all we can to avoid that same problem.

Pray again.

Several Christian organizations over the years have adopted a special saying that has been a help to millions. *"Much prayer, much power. Little prayer, little power."* As Paul said, God's strength is made perfect in our weakness or our averageness. When it comes to brute strength, the nation Israel has never been a super-power. If boxing terms were our measuring stick, Israel would be known as a flyweight.

Nevertheless, history abounds with stories of how Israel has survived through the most incredible mismatches in size and power when there was little potential for victory. Only God's divine hand has spared His people from extinction time after time.

That same God is the God who lives in us Christians today. Our honest, faithful, transparent prayers can bring us into the presence of Almighty God who, though He could slay us, chooses to add power to ours and leads us onward.

Think you are just average? God is saying, "*Come and go to the head of the class!*" There's nothing average about anybody if that means being barely noticeable and without purpose. God treats all those in his family as special, not because we deserve it, but because we're his kids. That matters!

The Abnormal

Jerry

The computer was still a rather new device in 1969 and personal computers were hardly an idea as yet. The large banks of hardware in the computer lab at Taylor University where I attended would today look like a scene from an old science fiction movie.

Nevertheless, I needed to endure a computer class my junior year if I was to graduate. Unfortunately, I was not just supposed to learn to use a computer, but how to program it as well.

Twice each week I would venture forth into the lab with my punch cards in hand (remember keypunching anyone?) and a printout of my program hoping that it would run smoothly from beginning to end. It rarely did.

More often than not my work would come to a grinding halt part way through the run, signaling an error somewhere within the hundreds of steps I had written.

It was in those times that I learned to appreciate Jerry who served as the lab assistant several days a week. But Jerry wasn't your normal assistant, waiting to help students as he sauntered through the room or while studying by himself in a glass-walled office.

No, Jerry, was severely handicapped, confined to a small, somewhat deformed body with an oversized head. He spent his life laying on a hospital-style gurney, his breathing helped by a tube that constantly laid on his lower lip.

I never observed Jerry walking or playing ball. He couldn't. I never saw Jerry use his arms to hug a child or friend. But I never heard Jerry gripe either. Instead he graduated from Taylor with honors. I saw him obtain a job of importance, being useful in spite of his abnormalities.

I didn't really know Jerry that well but I will never forget those moments in the computer lab when my program would quit for the tenth time in a row and I would say, "*Jerry, I need help!*"

He would always respond with a little chuckle and say something like, "*Okay, Gary, bring it over here and let me look at it.*"

I would humbly deliver my wad of computer paper to his bed on wheels and hold the sheets over his chest so he could begin scrolling down the page with his eyes.

Mere moments later he would say with an uncritical laugh, "*I see your problem. Take a look at line 350 . . . .*" Soon I was on my way to a working program.

If Jerry had lived only for *someday*, he would have had to wait until Heaven where he is today to enjoy life or find purpose. And certainly, Heaven is a wonderful experience for Jerry as he lives without the restrictions that his fleshly prison kept him in for so long.

But Jerry knew that life begins where we're at, in the *NOW*, not on the day when everything is normal, or as it should be by someone's standards. From that two by six-foot bed, Jerry radiated life and the knowledge that he could make a difference in the world.

Though Jerry's physical chains were heavy, his heart was free, full of life and energy for whatever opportunities God gave him to serve others.

In contrast, many Christians use their differences or abnormalities as an excuse to be a slave to the *Someday Syndrome.*

The widowed mother feels lonely now and longs for companionship, fellowship and a sense of purpose. She is embarrassed at the multitude of hateful thoughts she has contemplated over the years toward couples and families who are still intact, unbroken by the chisel of death.

If she would only begin to see her state as an opportunity for service, change and growth, and allow herself to enjoy the freedom she has to help others, she could be a new person! Of course, she must grieve and do so deeply for an extended time. That's normal.

And yet God has always been a God of life, not death. He can take a once normal wife and transform her into an abnormal, yet giving, caring, feeling woman. God might open an opportunity for her to lead a support group for other widows, help single moms with childcare or direct a Bible study of women during her lunch hour at work. The possibilities are endless.

Who knows what the Lord might have envisioned for her, even though she is now considered abnormal, at least by some, because she no longer has a spouse?

I'll never forget a scene from the powerful, riveting, and now decades old film series, *Whatever Happened to the Human Race?*, by Franky and Francis Schaeffer. The camera was focused close on the face of a handsome young man in his early twenties, highlighted with dark, wavy hair, a jutting chin and sparkling eyes.

He spoke articulately, sitting on the beach with the sound of the waves crashing around him. He spoke confidently how he was enjoying life and that God was using him in such incredible ways. He continually told the interviewer that he was so glad to be alive!

Those words would seem normal from a handsome young guy in such a beautiful spot but soon a lump came to my throat as the camera panned away from its portrait position.

It was then that we saw that this radiant personality and lover of life had no arms and no legs! His purpose for living clearly came from within, not from his outward appearance or lot in life.

His contemporary counterpart is a young man named Nick Vujicic whose testimony inspires thousands each year. Nick was born with no arms or legs and yet shares a vibrant, powerful story of how God is using him and others who don't fit the normal label.

Somehow these men make the words of the Psalmist David in chapter 139 take on a new depth and richness: *"For you created my inmost being; you knit me together in my mother's womb. I praise you because I am fearfully and wonderfully made; your works are wonderful; I know that full well. (vv. 13-14)*

Oh, how the church needs more Jerrys, Moses', Pauls, Nicks and others who feel like misfits. What is abnormality anyway?

Do you remember when you were in grade school or junior high and how you feared so desperately that you would do something that would make you look different? We always had to wear the right shoes, bring the stylish lunch box, or have only the coolest shirt or sweatshirt.

We learned early on that being different or abnormal had the potential to inflict pain, embarrassment or separation. And even worse, those social standards changed rapidly making it a constant battle to remain in the "in" crowd and avoid rejection.

We all know the damage that what we call bullying today still does.

If we are going to overcome our paralysis due to our perceived abnormality, then we must begin to see ourselves as God sees us, special and uniquely qualified to do a job that no one else can do as well as we can.

We must remember what David said in Psalm 139:1, *"O Lord, you have searched me and you know me."* God's view of us must be our only standard for normal. In fact, I love the title of a book by John Ortberg, *Everybody's Normal 'Til You Get To Know Them.*

Advertising, models, Hollywood, and television all tell us what normalcy is, but in reality God sets the norms! Our abnormalities may still cause us pain at times. Some people will not always accept us as we are.

We may face huge obstacles because of our deficiencies. However, God is the Sovereign God of whom Jeremiah says, "*Nothing is too difficult for Thee.*"

Scores of the church's greatest leaders, writers, and missionaries saw their ministries flourish from humble, even strange beginnings and circumstances.

John Bunyon wrote his famous *Pilgrim's Progress* while languishing in a Bedford jail for twelve years! John Milton wrote the renowned epic poem, *Paradise Lost*, suffering blindness, loneliness and poverty.

George Whitefield, one of the great preachers of the18th century, had a tavern-keeper for a father, and grew up surrounded by immorality and decadence. Dwight L. Moody's father died when he was but four years old and Dwight did not even trust Christ until he was eighteen years

We need to begin to understand that God often sees our abnormalities as advantages, characteristics that deepen our understanding of pain, sin and helplessness, and widen our vision and insight into the hurts of those God would have us minister to.

Would you hire this man to work for you? At age twenty-two his business failed. At twenty-three, he ran for office and lost. At twenty-four, he failed again in business. At twenty-five, he was finally elected to the Legislature. At twenty-six, his sweetheart died. At twenty-seven, he had a nervous breakdown. From twenty-nine to thirty-one, he lost his next three elections.

After being elected to Congress, he lost his next three elections, the last during his forty-ninth year of life. Abnormal, dysfunctional? Perhaps? A loser? Consider him anyway. His name was Abraham Lincoln!

Joni Eareckson Tada, a quadriplegic, has for decades encouraged other handicapped people. Chuck Colson, jailed because of his Watergate involvement, developed a world-wide prison ministry. Nicki Cruz, a former gang member, worked for years with inner-city drug addicts. Gladys, a former widow in my church, led a small group of single moms.

Of course, God does not require that our past struggles be the focus of our future ministry. Many of the leaders discussed earlier are examples of that. For some a return to fellowship with people from the past or similar to those of earlier days will burden with an emotional load that we may not be ready to bear without more time to heal.

Nevertheless, in many cases, our impairments, past or present, may be the tools that give our ministry power, life and effectiveness.

"I will be glad and rejoice in your love; for you saw my affliction and knew the anguish of my soul. You have not handed me over to the enemy but have set my feet in a spacious place. (Psalm 31: 7,8)

What place does God have for you? David spoke of, *Speaking before kings and not being ashamed!* (Psalm 119: 46) However, be careful! If you ask God to use you, even with your perceived disabilities, He will likely answer. Be ready!

Rahab, the harlot, was prepared when God called upon her to care for the spies, Joshua and Caleb. She is even listed in the Bible's, *Faithful Hall of Fame,* in Hebrews 11 and is part of the genealogy of Jesus!

Give your abnormality to God

Admit to God that you have been hiding behind those things as a way to avoid changing and becoming all God wants you to be. Face the hurt you have felt in wanting to be more like others or somebody else.

It's likely that you really wanted to be those things so someone would love you more or think more of you. You believed that your abnormalities were keeping you from what you wanted so much, to be loved and matter.

As anthropologist Margaret Mead said, "*One of the oldest human needs is having someone wonder where you are when you don't come home at night.*" Go back to chapters seven and eight and review those important biblical concepts and how to begin to change.

Take each of the qualities or circumstances on your list and ask God to help you begin to see it as an advantage. Sometimes psychologists call this *reframing.* If you put a different frame around a picture, it can suddenly look very different.

The same concept works for our view of our personal deficiencies. Try and see yourself through God's eyes and ask God how you might use your history, even with all its difficulties, hurts and frustrations and turn it into something good. Place God's frame of love, compassion and personal attention around every detail of your conception, creation and development.

Remember, affliction is rarely a godly excuse to embrace uselessness. Listen to David once again as he faces the reality of his own internal conflicts: *"Hear, O Lord, and answer me, for I am poor and needy. Guard my life, for I am devoted to you. You are my God; save your servant who trusts in you."* (Psalm 86: 1, 2)

Zecharias and Elizabeth had no children for a time and yet Luke 1: 6 tells us, *"And they were both righteous in the sight of God, walking blamelessly in all the commandments and requirements of the Lord."*

In both scenarios God saw afflicted people who were still worthy in His eyes, even godly. Christians need to come to grips with their deepest sin being that they didn't trust God for their worthiness, value and love, not that they have somehow fallen short of God's standard.

Your abnormalities can become advantages if you place them into God's hands for his shaping, molding and rearranging. What will you lay at His feet today, perhaps for the very first time? Maybe what you need to offer God is simply your *uniqueness, your specialness,* that only you can be right now.

The Antagonistic Toward God

My student Doug, who I introduced at the beginning of the chapter, was at times hostile towards God and most forms of authority. Many of his zany antics were his way of saying, *"I'm not interested in what you want me to do. I'm going to do my own thing, thank you."*

But he had his special moments, too. You could like Doug some of the time, even when his niceness was manipulative. However, there are some individuals who frankly are just mad about life! God or life or fate or whatever they happen to refer to it dealt them a bad hand and they are going to be miserable, critical, obnoxious, and repulsed by any form of love, compassion or caring.

In a few cases they will go out of their way to denounce God, defame Christians and biblical principles while acting out in ways to make you even more disappointed in them.

The apostle Paul, while still known as Saul, was one such antagonist. He hated Christians and notoriously sought them out and imprisoned them, arranging for their death in many cases. (Acts 8:1-3; 9:1-2) Saul, however, could hardly be considered disadvantaged, average or abnormal.

He was privileged to have the foremost education gained at the feet of Gamaliel. He had risen through the ranks of Judaism with ease, zealous to uphold the traditions of his ancestors. (Galatians1: 13)

Nevertheless, Saul had no remorse observing the stoning of Stephan. He was spurred on to ravage the church and seek her destruction while it was still in its infancy. Of all the individuals God might have considered to flame the growth of His church throughout the world,

Saul was an unworthy candidate! How could someone so clearly against Christ ever be one of His disciples?

For some reason many people become enraged at God, driven to spite Him and hate the influence of those who personally followed His Son Jesus. Earlier we looked at people who are angry in general, but anger towards God has its own special dynamics:

Antagonistic people usually have an erroneous view of God.

They have heard that God is supposed to be loving, so they expect that a loving God always gives people what they want-happiness, pleasurable, nice feelings and positive circumstances. Instead of seeking to understand a complete God, one who is both totally just and totally loving, they only wish that He be loving.

And yet a bit of logical thinking and a brief look at scripture clearly show otherwise. A favorite question of skeptics for Christians is, "*If God is so loving why do good people die?*" What they are really assuming by that question is that God must be only loving, a premise which devalues and limits the character of God. What we must all understand is the complete character of God as described in Psalm 89:14:

"Righteousness and justice are the foundation of Thy throne: Lovingkindness and truth go before Thee."

The purpose of this book is not to develop a theological perspective of God so I must be brief here. Let it suffice to say that scripture as a whole unquestionably paints a picture of God that attempts to show mankind who He truly is. Not only is God loving, but He's also just.

Therefore, to answer the skeptic's question, God allows good people to die because He is also fair. If today He were to right the world of all its evil, then which of us would be left? We would all die!

As a result, God has chosen to continue to allow sinful acts to occur in a fallen world, all the while loving His children who have accepted Christ as their Savior.

Therefore, antagonistic people are really hoping to change God's character, to something which would make their world more pleasant and comfortable. In their minds, that sort of God would never have let them be taken advantage of by the former pastor or be terminated from a job they had given twenty-five years to or suffer the loss of a young child.

Antagonists are generally fearful of relationship

This is why responding to God for them is such a threat. I have never met a person who is angry at God who is concurrently experiencing a deep, meaningful, loving relationship with another person. All their associations are shallow and guarded at best.

I worked recently with a guy named Jason. Jason made you feel like you were his friend after knowing him only five minutes. In his short life of less than thirty years, Jason, however, had known divorce, job failures, a business failure, jail, alcoholism and drug abuse.

Admirably, he had been dry for a number of years and when I met him was trying to get things back together with his former wife and begin to grow spiritually for the first time in his life.

Thankfully, he did grow, but he always seemed to stay at a distance. Even those he was closest to would find him inching away from them by returning to old habits, limiting his associations, being irresponsible and the like.

Those who had shown him the greatest love became those he rejected first! I am convinced that Jason would not let himself be loved just as he was. That was too threatening and meant that he now owed something to the others.

How sad and yet how typical of so many people today. Antagonists get perks from their style of living.

Their open hostility towards a friend, spouse or associate allows them to keep Christ followers at arm's length. Control is essential, allowing them to avoid feeling or tasting the love and caring that deep down inside they long for. Their adversarial position helps them avoid the possibility that they might actually enjoy a believer's involvement.

And yet it is fallen people, like Jacob, who have wrestled with Almighty God that are often those who make the greatest impact on the kingdom in the long run. They have peered at God from many angles, questioned Him and His Word in detail and finally when their eyes and mind clear and they see God in all of His greatness, they come to Him eager to serve for the rest of their lives.

Why the sudden change? Well, obviously they must be touched by God Himself and receive Christ like the rest of us. But I believe that their stringent war against God forces them to ponder Him in a way that few of us ever do.

So much of the time we like to keep God nice and tidy. We know He is great, awesome and powerful and we do appreciate His forgiveness, but most of us have never stared contemptuously into His eyes with venom dripping from our lips.

Many antagonists have. I don't recommend that we copy them or suggest a service of contempt become an ordinance of the church. But I do believe that we need to pray diligently for those who we know who are enraged at God and look forward to the day when they too will become a devoted servant of His.

We need to trust God for opportunities to help move these friends away from their someday thinking - and toward a loving God who cares about them yet is still just and fair.

Sometimes a bright-light experience is needed as was the case with Saul. Often antagonistic individuals will need the words of a loving confronter, who with God's grace and help forces them to sit up straight and see the folly of their war against spiritual things.

If you yourself are angry with God, then I encourage you to find a friend, counselor, pastor, spouse, etc. to whom you can begin to freely discuss the specific sources of your animosity (family, abuse, rejection, ignorance, whatever.) I would also suggest that somewhere in this process you write down your feelings about God and bring them to Him. He's a God of grace, love and mercy.

Wherever you are on your journey, your meeting Him again, face to face, with your heart open can be a truly joyful, lifechanging experience. As David said in Psalm 51: *"The sacrifices of God are a broken spirit; A broken and a contrite heart, O God, You will not despise."* (v. 17) God can transform the energies used to war with Him into life-giving relationship and productive activities that glorify Him.

As I conclude this chapter, some of you may feel that much of what I have said is simply positive thinking. And you're right. Living NOW and not in the someday does require positive thinking. But I'm not suggesting a blue-sky mentality where we pretend all is well when Hell is breaking loose.

No, I'm talking about thinking that moves us to look at ourselves as God does, positively, with affection, looking past our sin because of Christ's death on the cross. When we see God in that light, we are free to bring our actions, attitudes, and deception to Him without running the other way.

We can endure shame, embarrassment, longing for love, guilt and all the other emotions we may fear because God will not run from us. He will still welcome us to Himself with open arms. That is far more than positive thinking. That's salvation!

Do you see yourself as an unlikely hero for God? Do your personal struggles with average-ness, abnormality, or antagonism towards God Himself continue to cloud your horizons and strangle any hope you might have for a fruitful, godly life?

Then choose to ask God right now to begin to touch your eyes as Jesus did for the blind man, helping you to see your being average as potential, your abnormality as an advantage and even your antagonism as a doorway to growth.

The church today needs every member of the body to move towards his or her full potential in Christ. *Someday* living will only result in a select few doing the majority of the work. The job is simply too big for that.

Things to Think About In Chapter 12

In your mind, which of the three A's describes you best?

What would you need to believe again that would allow you to legitimately embrace that label?

What could you say to yourself over and over the next two weeks that would solidify your understanding of who you are in Christ?

Read Psalm 18 and jot down any concepts that hit you hard, encourage you in a major way or build you up

PURSUING JOY NOW
CHAPTER 13

"The Bible says to serve the Lord with gladness. Let's go out all the
way. Let's serve him all the way with gladness."
Martin Burnham

When I was in seminary, I began a Bible study project that took several years to complete. Of course, like any good grad student, I did my regular classroom work but this was extra. My quest had been to find the meaning of the word *joy* using the Bible as my guide.

I began my journey by simply circling the word every time it appeared in any book, Old or New Testament, and then noting the context. I soon encountered some of the more familiar passages on joy; Psalm 51: 12, "*Restore unto me the joy of my salvation*," or Galatians 5:22, "*The fruit of the Spirit is love, joy, peace, ...*"

But it was only when I had catalogued hundreds of verses that I actually began to sense the broad scope of this fascinating, rich, yet often mysterious term. For example, I found that joy is often coupled with difficult circumstances.

James 1:2, "*Consider it all joy when you encounter various trials,*" is one such occurrence. Several passages speak of God *making our joy complete*, implying that joy can soothe an aching soul like little else. (John 3:29; I John 1:4; Philippians 2:2)

I also began to ponder times in my life when I believe I encountered real joy, not just a pleasant feeling or pleasurable circumstances, but something deeper and richer. Several examples came to my mind rather quickly.

First, I was fairly confident that I had faced joy when I observed and participated in the births of our two children. I am still grateful for the open doors of the hospital delivery room that allowed this dad to view the magnificent spectacle of birth, especially when my wife had Caesarean section deliveries both times.

As a songwriter and musician, I couldn't help but write down my thoughts at the time and put them to music. Here are the now forty-plus-year-old words to Tim's song which I think express why I sensed joy when he came into being:

MIRACLE

Verse 1
Today, I watched him come into this world, In pain, in crying and fright,
But as I saw this dear new life begin, I was sure it was all God's delight.

Chorus
I know I just saw a miracle,
This life born in love has begun,
And though I'll never understand it all,
Thank you Lord for this miracle you've done.

Verse 2
It's so hard to think that this little one is ours,
So small, so helpless, so new,
Help us, Lord, to love him with all of Your love,
And may he know your miracles, too.

Chorus repeat

Now, Lord, we humbly commit him to you,
For Your plan that you only know,
Help us lead and guide Him in Your Holy Word,
In Your strength may he ever grow.

Chorus repeat

©Gary Sinclair, 1978

Okay, so fundamentally this wasn't the best song I ever wrote but it meant a lot to Jackie and me. As each child entered this world, slimy, bloody, yet brimming with life, I wanted to shout out loud, "*Tell me there is no God!*"

To see how two cells were now multiplied trillions of times over to knit together a human tapestry, each part functioning with miraculous ease, is a joyful moment of epic proportion.

Second, unmistakable joy always came when I had the privilege of leading someone else to Christ. To watch another human transformed from a life or purposelessness, guilt and little hope to knowing without a doubt that they are a child of God, has always brought me something that has to be joy!

Scripture tells us that there is a similar joy among the angels when a new child enters the kingdom of God! (Luke 15: 7) Too few Christians have experienced this kind of life-changing moment.

However, a third kind of joy kept stalking me during my journey to find joy. But this time there weren't the euphoric feelings that came with the first two examples. No, in setting three I am returning to God, broken, guilt-laden and overwhelmed that I can receive God's unfailing love and His open arms welcoming me back. I've messed up again and need his forgiveness, but He doesn't walk away.

Though I fear His rejection, He not only receives me but also pursues me. He wants me in His presence and enjoys being with me! While I didn't know it the first time, I would later understand it like Zephaniah did, His rejoicing over me with singing. (Zephaniah 3:17) It was in this very different setting that I learned that I could experience the greatness of God and taste joy.

Picture yourself in a hospital bed, broken, bruised and barely recognizable due to significant swelling and numerous other wounds. I'll never forget one such young lady who I visited in the hospital, not recognizing her at first because of the severity of her bruised and battered face. In our fictitious example, your friends and relatives come to visit but you sense they want to quickly leave, uncomfortable with your hideous appearance.

In fact, you detect that others are also repulsed by your condition, even though you long for them to stay and be with you.

Before long the visiting hours are over and you lay there alone and silent. Tears stream down your cheeks, your heart crying out for one friend or family member to be with you. Could you really have been that ugly? If only someone cared deeply enough to stick around in spite of your abhorrent exterior?

However, you finally detect a movement in the room and sense that someone is there. A figure looms in the shadows but you find yourself unafraid. Within seconds the unknown one steps into the light and you immediately recognize Jesus Himself. His eyes radiate warmth, his smile is real and gentle and His hand reaches out to touch your arm.

There is no sign of disgust or is He restless and eager to go as your friends seemed to be. Your heart melts as the Master says, "*Child, I still love you, in spite of it all. No, I will never leave you or forsake you.*"

A surge of emotion overtakes you and tears of happiness stream from your eyes, your hands reaching blindly for the nail-scarred ones of Jesus. What do you feel? I think that's joy, too! Only the greatness of God's love would be enough to love you at that moment without condition or reason. He sees the depths of our sinfulness and yet chooses to stay anyway.

You see, joy isn't the heightening of pleasure or the accumulation of more happy moments. Joy is best realized as we plumb the depths of our destitution before God and yet hear Him say, "*I can still use you for My purposes if you are willing.*" Isn't that what many in scripture said to Jesus, "*If you are willing, Lord . . .*" and were then told by the Master what great faith they had?

Jesus didn't want their talents first. He wanted their honesty and faith that He could make them whole no matter how bad they were.

If only more Christians knew real joy. If only more believers knew how to live openly and honestly in the unconditional love of Christ. Our churches would be overrun with loving, authentic, involved people, who were radically impacting the world in which they live, work and play.

They would be entrusting their lives into the hands of a compassionate God, looking to see His greatness in their imperfect lives. And the result is joy. In fact, others would likely want to know where their joy came from.

But instead, many Christ followers are controlled by depression, anxiety, pity, or discouragement. Many believers look great on the outside while paralyzed by boredom, niceness, and tradition, wondering when they lost their joy.

Could it be that our joy has declined because we trust less and less in the grace and greatness of God? How many churches today are actually asking God to perform ministry that is bigger than they are?

How many believers are stuck in the mire of *someday* thinking keeping them from risking their lives in service for God? How many congregations send the message each week, *"Only healthy and together people are wanted here."*

Once as I stood atop an eighty-foot cliff, clinging only to a rappelling rope, I learned another vital lesson about joy. Our guide had tied me onto the rope and was giving me my last-minute instructions since I had never rappelled before. My feet were firmly planted on the edge of the cliff and my hands were solidly grasping the rope ahead of me and behind my back.

And yet I was going nowhere at that point! It was then that the guide spoke these scary, but important words, *"You have to lean back."*

Lean back? Doing that would mean I had to stare at the ground, the place of certain death if the rope broke. But it was only when I began to lean back and place myself completely under the rope's power that I began to enjoy the thrill of travelling down the side of that cliff.

When I reached the ground, my heart racing and my hands shaking, I desired only one thing. To return to the top and do it again! I found joy in the presence of my terror! Exhilaration in the presence of inadequacy.

It's that same *exhilarating terror* the church must embrace today! It will only be aroused, however, when individual believers begin to seek joy that results from experiencing the greatness of God. And the result is often that we start to enjoy more exhilaration and less terror when we do tough things!

Prerequisites of Finding JOY

So, what might it take to embrace authentic joy? In church gatherings, some would suggest that more upbeat and contemporary services are signs that joy is on the rise. Others would argue for deeper, exegetical Bible teaching and extended periods of prayer and meditation to fuel joy in the church.

The extremes are clearly evident in churches today. On the one end of the spectrum are the hand-raising, exuberant services punctuated with hallelujahs and other free expression often used as measures of joyful congregations.

Anybody who doesn't join in may be labeled as *not in the Spirit*. The opposite extreme can lead others to believe that joy is purely personal and should be kept to oneself. This group thinks that heartfelt expressions of emotion should be left to God and the person.

However, joy is far more complex and richer than either extreme would suggest. Let me offer what seem in Scripture to be fundamentals for finding joy as God offers it.

A refined idea of JOY.

First of all, joy is not happiness in greater supply. Joy is no doubt a feeling, but not mere emotion. Joy requires a new mindset that looks at life as God sees it, even when our feelings are unpleasant. Proverbs reminds us: *"Even in laughter the heart may ache, and joy may end in grief. (14: 13)*

Joy requires that we expose our souls and our bodies to God who is also capable of killing us on the spot. It is in those sometimes painful, often devastating moments that we will encounter real joy when He chooses to love us anyway.

"Those who sow in tears shall reap with joyful shouting." *(Psalm 126:5)*

Terry Anderson, the Iranian hostage who decades ago was held for nearly seven years, said this following his release:

"We come closest to God at our lowest moments. It's easiest to hear God when you are stripped of pride and arrogance, when you have nothing to rely on except God. It's pretty painful to get to that point, but when you do, God's there."

Joy can no longer be something we require from outside of ourselves but instead be a reality that springs up within us as God's Holy Spirit exposes our weaknesses but transforms us anyway. At times joy will be a powerful, outward expression while at other times a sense that all is well, that the walls are not crashing down even though our lives seem to be crumbling.

When Jackie was diagnosed with colon/rectal cancer, she was sent to the hospital to receive a Groshong or port to be placed in her upper chest. This port would receive the medications she would need during the next several months.

However, during the procedure the doctor accidentally nicked her lung and she ended up back in the hospital with a tube in her chest for the next several days.

As I headed to an important Christmas rehearsal that evening, I found my eyes filled with tears and heart overwhelmed at the thought of my soulmate not only having cancer but enduring this latest ordeal that wasn't even her fault!

I remember telling God that I needed His Spirit to pray a Romans 8 prayer for me right then with groanings and words I didn't have. It was just as I said those words that I looked over at the SUV turning the corner next to me and saw the license plate. It said, PRAYIN' 7.

While the pain during that time was intense, God seemed to say that He was still enough and had not left me. I believe I experienced joy that night too.

Joy is an inward, powerful sense of peace that God is sufficient whether we are locked within the worst of circumstances or freely enjoying God's richest blessings.

The sensing of joy can never be dependent on our circumstances but rather on encountering the greatness of God. What we often call joy is a temporary, reachable happiness that feels good for the time being but doesn't have its home deep within us like joy does.

Challenges bigger than we are.

As you have read this book, I hope you have seriously considered the next steps you might take to become more like Christ. Those changes may seem like mountains in the light of your present circumstances or past history. The idea of serving God with all your heart, soul and mind, may seem like an undeserved privilege for someone like you.

And yet, nonetheless, God has called you to a life of radical service for Him not dependent on heritage, ability, or class. He is asking you to become part of the task of impacting the world for Christ. Some of us will travel to other countries, others will simply walk across our lawns to our neighbors' homes.

Many will rub shoulders with coworkers while others will be Christ in volunteer work, caring for the needy and encouraging those who are hurting.

Like Nehemiah, we must be convinced that as a child of God we have the privilege to be passionately involved in a great work reaching our world for Christ. To get there will at times seem bigger than we are or that we have settled for something too easy.

When we were rappelling, we could have used a six-foot cliff and called it rappelling but we would have missed the challenge of doing something larger. There would have been little excitement in conquering a route no taller than we were.

How big of a challenge are you willing to trust God for? Will you let your personal deficiencies keep you from what you are capable of doing? Remember if joy is dependent on experiencing the greatness of God, then the greater the challenge, the more we'll experience Him!

God-sized risks.

Very few enjoy being in the presence of someone foolhardy. And yet many people die each year because they take unnecessary risks. Some daredevils are even thought to have a death-wish mentality, enamored with the idea of brushing the face of eternity.

The movie, *Free Solo,* chronicles the 3000-foot free climb of Alex Honnold up *El Capitan* in Yosemite. He had no ropes, no harness, no safety net. And while he was incredibly trained and prepared, the risks were high even for him. And yet, he also did something no one else had ever done.

When I speak of being a risk-taker, I'm not talking about being foolish or trying to tackle the wildest thing we can imagine just for the fun of it. That wasn't Alex Honnold's goal either. I am, however, thinking of radical actions that fly in the face of natural logic and go where many others won't go.

To experience true joy, we must plunge into the waters of our worst fears like rejection, being unloved, failure, appearing incompetent in front of those who matter most to us. We must be like the bungee jumper who plummets to the earth with increasing velocity, wondering whether these are the final moments of life when the cord snaps and life is over.

Joyful people are jumpers. They're willing, though nervous, to hurl themselves headlong towards the fears that at one time ruled them. They know they must live beyond the knowledge of the rope's holding power and experience firsthand the strength of the lifeline that will protect them. Joy seekers aren't paralyzed by fear.

Although I've never bungee-jumped, I do know that there comes a point in which the jumper realizes for sure that he or she is safe. At that point their heart rate lessens and the butterflies in the stomach recede.

In the same way, the Christian life involves a similar *terror followed by peace* when we find that our challenges and new ventures weren't fatal. But God doesn't always keep us from the initial fear. His rope of love around our legs doesn't necessarily mean we'll avoid rejection, criticism or personal attack. It does mean He will still hold onto us so that our worth won't be destroyed no matter how dreadful our circumstances.

It is God's staying with us that encourages us to try the risky, joy-producing behavior again.

The next time our fear will decrease as the security of the rope takes hold. Nevertheless, the uneasiness can remain for a while and the fears might be faced again. We must repeatedly be held by the power of the rope before our worries ebb to where they control us less and empower us more.

Such is Christian living much of the time. Many speakers and seminar leaders would like us to believe that the process is far simpler, that godliness is easily attained and lived out. But that is rarely the case.

If godliness were easy, then how meaningful and essential to life could it be? David said in II Samuel 24:24, *"I will not sacrifice to the Lord my God burnt offerings that cost me nothing."* Should we do any less?

When we get used to trusting God for results bigger than we are, our faith and trust in Him always grow. We start thinking big instead of just getting by, the impossible not just the possible.

Joy becomes more normal and everyday even when God's asking us to do BIG things.

Accepting joy's limits in this life.

Although I've spoken of experiencing joy, we have to accept that it's limited and not complete just yet. Pure joy can never be our ultimate goal here.

There are some reasons for this disappointing reality. First of all, when we experience joy, we are encountering a bit of heaven. I have always been enamored with the words of David in Psalm 34, *"Taste and see that the Lord is good; blessed is the man who takes refuge in Him."* (v. 7)

Much of what we experience as blessings in this life are tastes of joy this side of Heaven.

Hearing the *Hallelujah Chorus* always seems to me to be a powerful example of a heavenly taste. Seeing a pink, smiling, new born baby is another tiny picture of life to come in eternity. Viewing a mountainous panorama feels like a still photograph of a part of Heaven that will welcome us home someday.

Unfortunately, none of these thrilling moments here on earth lasts. Handel's *Hallelujah* is soon drowned out by the deafening sounds of everyday life. The newborn grows up to be one of us, not the perfect little bundle we once held. Our vacation to the mountains ends and we must return to the cold, sterile sights and sounds of the city or farm.

In addition, think what it would be like to experience joy all the time. Our bodies aren't ready for that! That's likely why in heaven we will have new bodies, (I Corinthians 15), ones that can embrace all the wonders of heaven one hundred percent of the time.

You see, joy in this life must be a *result* not a goal, the outcome of passionate commitment to God regardless of our circumstances. We can taste joy now, but the best is yet to come.

Paul undoubtedly understood this when he spoke in II Timothy of longing to be at home with the Lord. He was ready to taste all the joy now, his body tired and worn out from wrestling with the cares and stresses of human life. And yet he needed to stay here a bit longer.

If anything, we'll experience more sadness than happiness in this life. No, I don't mean that Christians should live a morbid, disappointed life. Instead, *we must face the sadness that nothing in this world is ever enough to satisfy us.*

Our precious children, committed marriages, fulfilling jobs, degrees, accomplishments and ministries will all let us down. They will satisfy us for a while but like the

Novocain I spoke of earlier, its effects will wear off. Our sadness will remind us that hope is ultimately in the Lord, not in this world.

As Psalms says, *joy will come in the morning*. Many people spend lifetimes waiting, wondering when better feelings will arrive. Sadly, they have been lured into *Someday Syndrome* living. But God is calling the church, all Christians who know Christ as Savior, to live as people of NOW, serving God and sharing the message of the Gospel throughout life as they know it.

Paralysis, spiritual and cultural rigor mortis overtake God's people when they choose to remain stuck in their maladies, selfishness, fears, and excuses.

How much more exciting is the prospect that the church will grow and lead a significant movement here and around the world because Christians live for Christ NOW rather than waiting for some future result to occur first?

Will you be one of those who start or continue a NOW life right where you are? Don't wait. You have work to do and purposes to fulfill today. Beat the *Someday Syndrome.* Go, serve, grow and be who you were meant to be **NOW**!

FINAL THOUGHTS

So, you made it to the end of the book or shall I say *the top of the mountain!* Way to go. I hope you've gained tremendous insight about moving forward, setting aside your distractions and becoming the person you were meant to be *NOW*.

Would you do a big favor for me? Would you go to Amazon.com and write a review of the book there? Those reviews really matter in future sales and impact. Your help will invite even more people to be read *NOW*. Thanks.

Also, be sure to think about your next steps as a result of reading this book. You can start somewhere but whatever you do, please don't just put the book down and forget what you've learned. Let it make a difference in you by talking with others about what has impacted you NOW!

And to help you get started, list some of your key next steps below and then get going, even on just one. You're going to make a difference! In fact, I'd love to hear from you to know just what steps you took and how it went.

And if you don't mind, please write a review on Amazon.com by just clicking on my book there to do do so. Thanks so much for reading NOW!

NOW!

Other Books By Gary Sinclair

Turn Up Or Turn Around Your Parenting, 2014

Turn Up Or Turn Around Your Marriage, 2016,

Never Quit Climbing: Overcoming Life's Seemingly Insurmountable Mountains, 2019

Available at Amazon.com in paperback and eBook and possibly audiobook.

Follow or contact Gary to comment or for speaking and coaching through Facebook, Twitter, LinkedIn and Instagram or at www.neverquitclimbing.com.

Made in the USA
Columbia, SC
11 March 2022